PRAISE FOR *PERENNIAL SELLER*

"I said this about Ryan Holiday's last book, but I'll say this now about this book. This is his best book. This will be a perennial seller. Everything in here is so true and it is a guide to creativity in the real world."
—James Altucher, bestselling author of *Choose Yourself*

"As a showrunner or any kind of artist, you have to know when to stick to your guns and trust your gut, when and whom to ask for help, and how to define and lean into your brand. This book gets to the core of each of those elements in an attempt to help creatives be successful for a long time." —David Zuckerman, television writer and cocreator of *Family Guy, American Dad,* and *Wilfred*

"My first book took five years for it to become a bestseller. It sells more now than it did ten years ago. You won't find a better guide to create something that lasts than Perennial Seller! Ryan Holiday is one of the great marketing minds of our time!"
—Jon Gordon, bestselling author of *The Energy Bus*

"In an era of disposable hot takes, Ryan's writing blends thoughtful and thorough contrarianism with delicious anecdotes to back it up. *Perennial Seller* continues that tradition."
—Ricky Van Veen, cofounder *CollegeHumor* and *Vimeo,* head of global creative strategy at Facebook

"Ideas are a dime a dozen, but those who put them into practice are priceless. [In Perennial Seller], Ryan shows you how to become one of "those" through his simple and cutthroat strategy for what it takes to be a successful creative in the modern world. This book couldn't be more timely!" —Jake Udell, founder of TH3RD BRAIN; manager of Grace VanderWaal, Gallant, ZHU, and Krewella

"Every artist aspires to create timeless, lasting work and this book is a study on what it takes to do just that. Ryan Holiday has written a brilliant, inspiring guide to ignoring the trends of the day to focus on what matters and what will lead to real impact. If you want to write, produce, or build something amazing, read this book."
—James Frey, bestselling author of *A Million Little Pieces* and *Bright Shiny Morning*

"Fashion, like most industries, is all about what's popular right now, yet at the same time the best designers and creators aspire to make and sell things that will last more than just a single season. Holiday's new book is the ultimate road map to making your work and your message stick."
—Aya Kanai, chief fashion director for *Cosmopolitan*, *Seventeen*, *Redbook*, and *Woman's Day*

"Ryan Holiday is more than a marketing genius—he is an extraordinary thinker whose instincts deliver him deep into the human condition. I've been lucky to work with Ryan, and his goal is unwavering—to help creators make work that lasts. *Perennial Seller* is the perfect distillation of his ideas, and that rarest of gifts—a road map to success and an insight into life."
—Robert Kurson, *New York Times* bestselling author of *Shadow Divers*

"Autodidact extraordinaire Ryan Holiday strips away the ridiculous obsession with contemporary bestsellerdom and gets to the heart and soul of individual genius, creating timeless classics that change people's lives year after year after year. For those of us who wish to summon the courage and forgo instant validation in favor of deep and original creation, this book offers not just the Why, but the How. A must-read for creators of all persuasions."
—Shawn Coyne, cofounder of Black Irish Books, author of *The Story Grid: What Good Editors Know*

"At this moment, it's easy to think of music as no more than ephemeral content. For this reason, it's more important than ever to make work that stands the test of time. This book is a complete and current handbook for writing classics. *Perennial Seller* clears a path through the noise. If you are interested in creating work that stands the test of time, then *Perennial Seller* is a must-read."
—Justin Boreta, The Glitch Mob

"In a shortsighted culture obsessed with *virality*, it's refreshing to read a book concerned with *vitality*. How do we make an release creative works that it has a better chance of taking on a life of its own when it's out in the word? Once again, Ryan Holiday proves to be a writer worth stealing from."
—Austin Kleon, *New York Times* bestselling author of *Steal Like an Artist*

PERENNIAL SELLER

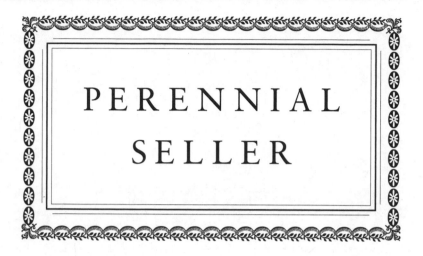

PERENNIAL SELLER

The Art of Making and Marketing Work That Lasts

RYAN HOLIDAY

FOUNDER OF BRASS CHECK

PORTFOLIO/PENGUIN

Portfolio/Penguin
An imprint of Penguin Random House LLC
375 Hudson Street
New York, New York 10014
penguin.com

Most Portfolio books are available at a discount when purchased in quantity for sales
promotions or corporate use. Special editions, which include personalized covers, excerpts,
and corporate imprints, can be created when purchased in large quantities. For more
information, please call (212) 572-2232 or e-mail specialmarkets@penguinrandomhouse
.com. Your local bookstore can also assist with discounted bulk purchases using the
Penguin Random House corporate Business-to-Business program. For assistance in
locating a participating retailer, e-mail B2B@penguinrandomhouse.com.

ISBN 9780143109013 (hardcover)
ISBN 9781101992142 (ebook)

Printed in the United States of America
1   3   5   7   9   10   8   6   4   2

Book design by Daniel Lagin

CONTENTS

❧❀❧

INTRODUCTION ✳ 1

Part I
THE CREATIVE PROCESS
From the Mindset to the Making to the Magic ✳ 15

Part II
POSITIONING
From Polishing to Perfecting to Packaging ✳ 61

Part III
MARKETING
From Courting to Coverage, Pushing to Promotion ✳ 107

Part IV
PLATFORM
From Fans to Friends and a Full-Fledged Career ✳ 173

CONCLUSION
What's Luck Got to Do with It? ✳ 219

AFTERWORD ✳ 229

A GIFT FOR YOU ✳ 231

ACKNOWLEDGMENTS AND SOURCES ✳ 232

INDEX ✳ 243

INTRODUCTION

❧❦❧

In 1937, a British literary critic named Cyril Connolly sat down to write a book around an unusual question: How does an author create something that lasts for ten years? Connolly's view was that the mark of literary greatness lay in standing the test of time. With the specter of world war looming on the horizon, the idea of anything surviving in an uncertain future had a kind of poignancy and meaning to it.

The book that Connolly wrote, *Enemies of Promise*, explored contemporary literature and the timeless challenges of making great art. It was also an honest self-examination of why Connolly, himself a talented writer, hadn't broken through commercially with his previous work. By no means a mainstream book, *Enemies of Promise* was still a provocative inquiry into the important questions that artists have always asked themselves and one another.

Considering the author's belief that he was qualified to determine what contributes to *lasting* work, we are faced with an interesting set of questions: How did his own work do? How long did a book about lasting end up surviving? Was he able to hit the mark he'd set? Could Cyril Connolly, like some literary Babe Ruth, actually end up sending the ball where he had called it?

While it never became a trendy cultural sensation, this unusual book ultimately endured through wars, political revolutions, fads, divorces, new styles (which became old styles and were transplanted by newer styles), massive technological disruption, and so much else. It lasted first for a decade—in 1948, ten years after its release, *Enemies of Promise* was expanded and given its first reprinting. The book got the same treatment in 2008, some sixty years later, and here we are again talking about it today.

Connolly managed to do what few artists can do: He made something that stood the test of time. His words still hold up and are still read. Cyril was quotable in his day and he's quoted today. (Most famous are acrid quips like: "There is no more somber enemy of good art than the pram in the hall" and "Whom the Gods wish to destroy, they first call promising.") The book has far outlived him and almost everything else published around the same time, retaining for Connolly a cult following decades after his death. And most impressively, given the subject matter, this success wasn't some accident. Clearly he consciously sought this—and achieved it. Today, all this time later, his theories about the creative process remain relevant, at least to me, since they were the inspiration for the book you're reading right now.

Is that not the kind of lasting success that every creative person strives for? To produce something that is consumed (and sells) for years and years, that enters the "canon" of our industry or field, that becomes seminal, that makes money (and has impact) while we sleep, even after we've moved on to other projects?

The novels of James Salter have been described as "imperishable." A translator of the dissident writer Aleksandr Solzhenitsyn once observed that the man's writing possessed a certain "change-less freshness." One of Bob Dylan's biographers has pointed out that even though many of the musician's songs were written about momentous events in the 1960s, the music holds true and has "transcended his time." What phrases! What a way to express what so many of us would like to achieve. Not only us writers or musicians, but, in their purest form, every entrepreneur, designer, journalist, producer, filmmaker, comedian, blogger, pundit, actor, investor—anyone doing any kind of creative work—is attempting to do just that: to have impact and to survive.

Yet undeniably, most of us fail in that effort. Why? First, we must grant that it's really hard. Backbreakingly, you-might-end-up-in-a-nuthouse-if-you-think-about-it-too-much hard. Though I suspect that's not why most creatives fall far short of making work that lasts for even ten minutes, let alone ten years. The truth is that they never give themselves a real shot at it. They fail because, stra-tegically, they never had a chance. Not when almost every incen-tive, every example, every how-to guide they look to, even the cues they take from well-meaning fans and critics, leads them in the wrong direction.

It's hard to see how it could be otherwise when the top "thought leaders" and business "experts" deceive us with short-cuts and tricks that optimize for quick and obvious success. Cre-ators resort to hacking bestseller lists, counting social media shares, or raising huge amounts of investor capital far before they have a business model. People claim to want to do something that matters, yet they measure themselves against things that don't, and track their progress not in years but in microseconds. They want to make something timeless, but they focus instead on imme-diate payoffs and instant gratification.

During the creative process, too many are led astray by short-cuts. We claim to want to be more than a flash in the pan, but at no juncture do we stop and consider how to increase longevity and shelf life. Instead, we use whatever is hot, cool, trendy, and selling well as our benchmarks. As a result, we have to produce more, market harder, sell out worse. It's a treadmill, and it's getting faster by the day.

No wonder people think creative success is impossible. With this short-term mindset, it more or less is.

A Better Way, a New Model

In every industry—from books to movies to restaurants to plays and software—certain creations can be described as "perennial." By that I mean that, regardless of how well they may have done at their release or the scale of audience they have reached, these products have found continued success and more customers over time. They are the kind of art or products that we return to more than once, that we recommend to others, even if they're no longer trendy or brand-new. In this way, they are timeless, dependable resources and unsung moneymakers, paying like annuities to their owners. Like gold or land, they increase in value over time because they are always of value to someone, somewhere. In other words, they are not simply perennial; they are *perennial sellers*.

Take *The Shawshank Redemption*, for example. As a movie, it underwhelmed at the box office—never playing on more than a thousand screens and barely clawing back its production budget in gross ticket sales. But in the years since release, it has brought in more than $100 million. There are minor actors in that movie who receive $800-plus checks every month in residuals. Turn on your television this weekend and you will probably find the movie playing somewhere on some channel.

There is a restaurant right next to the Staples Center in Los Angeles called the Original Pantry Cafe that is open twenty-four hours a day, seven days a week, every day of the year . . . and has been since 1924 (it famously doesn't even have locks on the doors). Known simply as the Pantry to its devoted regulars, it has amassed over 33,000 consecutive days (and over 792,000 consecutive hours) of selling breakfast food and the occasional steak. Most mornings there is a line outside to get in. The only thing that's changed in ninety-three years are the prices, grudgingly increased due to a century of inflation. A few blocks away, there's Clifton's Cafeteria, a restaurant that's been serving diners since 1935 (and that partly inspired the whimsical personality of Disneyland). On its wall is the longest continuously running neon sign in the world—lit without fail for over seventy-seven years.

My favorite band growing up was the heavy metal group Iron Maiden. Despite getting little radio airplay, they have managed to sell more than 85 million albums over the course of a four-decade-long career. Even today, they regularly sell out shows of 30,000 or even 60,000 seats all over the world.* How can they beat Madonna in Spotify streams (her top five songs at 110 million streams vs. Iron Maiden's top five songs at 160 million streams)? How do they do it? How does that happen?

Not that selling actual music is the only way to be perennial in the music business. Have you ever seen a drummer playing Zildjian cymbals? If you've watched Dave Grohl (Foo Fighters and Nirvana), Keith Moon (The Who), or Phil Collins, you sure have. That company was founded in Constantinople in 1623. Zildjian has been making cymbals *for four centuries.*

---

* Lady Gaga knows: "I always used to say to people when they would say, 'Oh, she's the next Madonna': 'No, I'm the next Iron Maiden.' "

Fiskars, the scissor company, has been around since 1649. The high-end candle company Cire Trudon has been around since the seventeenth century. Trudon may have made its name supplying candles to the court of King Louis XIV and later to Napoleon, but it's still a growing company—Trudon opened its first New York City retail location in 2015.

Here's what's even crazier: Chances are those companies will still exist in ten years. Whatever changes I will have to make to this book in later editions, I have little doubt that, barring some tragedy, the Pantry, *Shawshank*, Iron Maiden, and Zildjian will still be going strong. They are examples of a phenomenon known in economics as the Lindy effect.* Named after a famous restaurant where showbiz types used to meet to discuss trends in the industry, it observes that every day something lasts, the chances that it will continue to last increase. Or as the investor and writer Nassim Taleb has put it, "If a book has been in print for forty years, I can expect it to be in print for another forty years. But, and that is the main difference, if it survives another decade, then it will be expected to be in print another fifty years. . . . Every year that passes without extinction doubles the additional life expectancy."

In other words, classics stay classic and become more so over time. Think of it as compound interest for creative work.

Brilliant financial minds have grasped this reality of the creative industries for some time. In the 1990s, the investment banker Bill Pullman created an investment vehicle that allowed owners of the rights to valuable songs to raise bonds based on the future income streams of those perennial assets. Today they're called

---

* Lindy's opened on Broadway in 1921 and has two locations in Manhattan to this day.

"Bowie Bonds," since the late David Bowie raised some $55 million off the royalties of his back catalog.*

In 1986, an entrepreneur named Ted Turner bought the movie studios MGM and United Artists for a little over $1.5 billion. Just three months later, struggling under the debt of the two studios, he decided to sell the companies off in pieces, a big chunk of them right back to the person he'd bought them from in what looked like a huge loss. In fact, it was one of the most brilliant moves in the history of the entertainment business. Turner kept MGM's film library and the television rights to classic films that included block-busters like *Gone with the Wind* but was largely made up of a block of solid films like *Network*, *Diner*, *Shaft*, and *The Postman Always Rings Twice*. Combined, these films would produce more than $100 million a year in revenue, and when Turner would go on to launch channels like Turner Network Television (TNT) and Turner Classic Movies (TCM), they would play nonstop. He built a multibillion-dollar empire on perennial sellers—not only right in front of people's noses, but while those people were turning *up their noses at him*. "What do you want with a bunch of old movies no one watches anymore?" they scoffed.

The brilliance of it is that perennial sellers—big or small—not only refuse to die or fade into oblivion; they grow stronger with each passing day. The works of Homer and Shakespeare, along with hundreds of other dead playwrights and philosophers— despite all being available for free online—still sell hundreds of thousands of copies per year. *Star Wars* isn't suddenly going to stop making money—in fact, the profits from the franchise are actually now accelerating, some forty years after conception. Nor is every "classic" a towering work of staggering genius. In

* How long was the Bowie Bond for? Ten years!

2015, catalog albums in the music industry—titles at least eighteen months or older—outsold all new releases for the first time in the history of the music business. The albums your parents grew up listening to, that record you liked in high school, the steady climbers that are just getting going after a slow start—they moved more units than all the chart-topping artists and hot singles combined.

A year and a half—that's not so long. Compared with what George Lucas or Shakespeare has done, ten years doesn't seem so long either. So why does it seem to be so hard to do? Why do so few seem to even try? And is this reluctance—or deliberate ignorance—not an opportunity for those of us who are fascinated by these artistic outliers to set out to create our own?

A Lifelong Fascination

When I was a teenager, everything I liked was old. My favorite bands had released their first albums before I was born and were still going strong decades later when I came around (and thankfully, the ones that are still alive still are). I remember picking up *The Great Gatsby* in high school for the first time and being shocked that something intended to be so timely—about the Jazz Age—could, more than a half century later, still feel so timeless. Even the movies I found myself watching and rewatching weren't in the theaters; they were on television—the so-called classic films.

Early in my career, I was a research assistant for Robert Greene, whose historic masterwork, *The 48 Laws of Power*, didn't hit the bestseller lists until a *decade* after its release. It has since sold more than a million copies and has been translated into dozens of languages. I would suspect that a hundred years from now people will *still* be reading it. The first book I worked on was *I*

Hope They Serve Beer in Hell, by controversial blogger Tucker Max. It received a $7,500 advance from a small publisher after being rejected by almost every other imprint in the business, yet went on to sell an upwards of 1.5 million copies and spend six consecutive *years* on the bestseller lists. A perennial seller and then some—the book celebrated its ten-year anniversary recently, and still moves roughly three hundred copies week in and week out.

I later became the director of marketing at American Apparel, where the company's bestselling styles were not new trendy fashion pieces but its classic T-shirts, underwear, and socks. The founder once told me his goal was to make clothes that people years in the future would still be buying in vintage clothing shops. It was this focus on well-made staple products, combined with creative and provocative marketing, that helped American Apparel sell hundreds of millions of garments in its two decades in business.

All of this was my education in the art of the perennial seller—how they work, what goes into them, and why they matter, from both a personal and a business standpoint. I applied this knowledge in the creation of my own company, Brass Check, which has carved out a niche pushing clients toward creating and marketing work to *last*. Authors we've worked with have sold more than ten million books, spent seven hundred weeks on bestseller lists, and been translated into close to fifty languages. Our past media clients, including outlets like the *New York Observer* and Complex, have become quiet traffic behemoths. One of the startups I advise is a *vinyl record club*—the definition of a business model (and, surprisingly, a medium) that has endured.

I've even tried to apply this contrarian thinking to my own writing. I don't believe I have created masterpieces that will last a thousand years, but I humbly submit that longevity has been the aim of my work. I've tried to model my own books on the perennial mindset and have started to see the results of those efforts. You wouldn't know it from the *New York Times* best-seller list, but in the years since they've been published, my books have sold more than four hundred thousand copies in more than twenty-five languages and continue to sell steadily day in and day out. These works may go out of print someday, but every morning that they stick around increases their chances through another evening.

How to make something last—whether it's for a few months more than the average or for a century—has been my lifelong fascination. It's also become a question central to my livelihood. Is there a common creative mindset behind work that lasts? How is it different from work that's popular one day, gone the next? How do such creators think about the vocabulary used to package their work? What kind of relationship do they have with their fans and followers? Is there a pattern to perennial sellers that we can learn from?

These questions are what led me to research and write this book. In the pages that follow, we're going to examine these questions in many forms, from many industries, from many eras. Not just the incredible amount of work that goes into the creation of works that stand the test of time. But how to position them. How to market them. How to build a career around them. And how to avoid falling for the seduction of short-term notability to focus on the real brass ring: long-term success and renown.

In my quest for answers, I've spoken to everyone from Craig Newmark of Craigslist fame to legendary music producer Rick Rubin to Jane Friedman, whose company Open Road publishes for the estates of timeless authors like Thomas Wolfe, Isaac Asimov, and H. G. Wells. I interviewed agents, marketers, publicists, entrepreneurs, business owners, and academics about how to make things that last. And I tested some of my findings within my own company, often with surprising results.

A Decade? A Century? That's Impossible!

Makers of great work are intimidating. It's easy for us to look at them and think: They are better than me. They're special. The gods must have smiled on them. Only geniuses can achieve that level of success, and only flashes of inspiration from the muses can spur it. It's all about the right person at the right time in the right place.

The number of people in the entertainment industry who have told me some version of "You could never do that today" while discussing certain classic shows and works of brilliance is both heartbreaking and mystifying. How uninspiring is that? How fatalistic and defeatist? Surely one way to ensure that creating amazing, lasting work is impossible is by convincing everyone that it cannot be done on purpose.

I've seen too many clients do it too many times to know that longevity isn't an accident. Anyone who studies the history of literature, film, or art can see that while luck is certainly an important factor, perennial success is also the result of the right decisions, the right priorities, and the right product. There are too many commonalities among perennial sellers across many different mediums and industries for luck to be the only factor. With the right mindset, the right process, and the right set of business strategies, you can increase the likelihood that your work will join the ranks of these classics. Their success can be your success.

Yet, too often, the approach of the average creator is to hope to get lucky. On top of that, we focus on all the wrong metrics for measuring our success and, in the process, actually diminish our chances for longevity. Making a beloved classic that lasts for a hundred years may seem like a tall order. Fine, put that aside. What if we start by just trying to make something that lasts longer than average?

Cut flowers can outlast movies that people have poured millions into. Investors dump businesses and businesses shed products faster than a deer sheds its antlers. The average NFL lineman has a longer career than a book is given time to find its legs.

Let's start by rejecting those flawed assumptions from the outset. Let's start by internalizing the best practices of those who've achieved intermediate and lasting success so we can give ourselves the best chance of joining the lofty perch of those who have made something truly perennial and timeless. Let's be truly ambitious.

To that end, this will not be another marketing book—though marketing will be an important part of it. Instead, this book examines every part of the process from the creative act to creating a legacy. It will teach you:

- How to make something that can stand the test of time
- How to perfect, position, and package that idea into a compelling offering that stands the test of time
- How to develop marketing channels that stand the test of time
- How to capture an audience and build a platform that stands the test of time

I personally love books, and a lot of my clients and readers are authors, so there will be a lot here about books (not a bad industry to study, by the way, with over $70 billion a year in revenue). But the ideas put forth in this book are in no way limited to authors.

We're all selling ideas. Whatever the form, the process is the same. And if we get really good at it and we think about it the right way, our idea can sell forever, an infinite number of times.

That's the dream. To matter, to reach, to last.

So let's go get it.

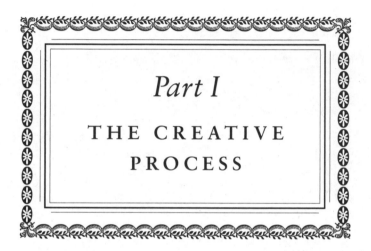

Part I

THE CREATIVE PROCESS

From the Mindset to the Making to the Magic

The more books we read, the clearer it becomes that the
true function of a writer is to produce a masterpiece and
that no other task is of any consequence.

—Cyril Connolly

A few years ago I got into an argument with a friend. This
person—whose company I enjoy and whose work I
respect—had declared the following to aspiring creatives
on Twitter: "You should spend 20 percent of your time creating
content and 80 percent of your time promoting it."

This kind of thinking sounds right. Lines like that are easy to
repeat at conferences and cocktail parties. It styles the speaker as
part of some bold new breed of creator, not one of the old, stodgy
dinosaurs. In its own way, it is inspiring too, saying: Don't over-
think it; just get out there and hustle!

There's only one problem: It's *terrible* advice.

So terrible that I know the successful entrepreneur who said it could never have gotten to where he is if he'd actually followed his own advice. He didn't have a large audience just because he was good at marketing—his successful marketing was dependent on the fact that he had a great product. Not only was he a counter-example of that very line of thinking, I can't say I know too many people whose success was built by spending one fifth of their time creating and four fifths loudly hawking the work they've just thrown together.

While there are many different types of success in this world, and prioritizing marketing and sales over the product may lead to some of them, that is not how perennial success is created. The kind of important, lasting work we are striving for is different— we're talking about making something that doesn't rely on hype or manipulative sales tactics. Because those methods aren't sustainable. And they do an injustice to great work.

Even as someone who loves the challenge and creativity and rigor of marketing, I'm alarmed at how many creators gloss over creating. They fritter away their time on Twitter and Facebook— not killing time, but believing that they are building up followers to be the recipients of their unremarkable work. They have meticulously crafted brands and impeccable personae crafted through media training. They spend money on courses and read books on marketing to develop sales strategies for products they haven't even made yet. All this churn may feel productive, but to what end?

To make something that will, *eventually*, disappear with the wind?

Even the best admen will admit that, over the long term, all the marketing in the world won't matter if the product hasn't been made right. In fact, it's a classic "measure once, cut twice" scenario, in that the better your product is, the better your marketing will be. The worse it is, the more time you will have to spend marketing and the less effective every minute of that marketing will be. You can count on that.

Promotion is not how things are made great—only how they're *heard* about. Which is why this book will not start with marketing, but with the mindset and effort that must go into the creative process—the most important part of creating a perennial seller.

The Work Is What Matters

The first step of any creator hoping for lasting success—whether for ten years or ten centuries—is to accept that hope has nothing to do with it. To be great, one must make great work, and making great work is incredibly hard. It must be our primary focus. We must set out, from the beginning, with complete and total commitment to the idea that our best chance of success starts during the creative process.

The decisions and behaviors that bring you to creating the product—everything you do before you sit down to build whatever it is you're building—trump any individual marketing decisions, no matter how attention-grabbing they turn out to be. And, as we'll see later, those creative decisions can be critical marketing decisions in themselves.

Crappy products don't survive. If you have phoned in the creative process, disrespected it, built a mediocre product, compromised, told yourself, "Hey, we'll figure the rest out later," then the project is likely doomed before it's even finished. The battle will be futile—and expensive. Look at basically everything Microsoft has made in the last decade—from the Zune to Bing. That poor company seems resigned to spending billions on marketing products that inevitably lose money. Meanwhile, Microsoft Office is still a cash cow after two and a half decades. I'm editing this book with it.

It's why all the pre-work matters so much. The conceptualization. The motivations. The product's fit with the market. The execution. These intangible factors matter a great deal. They cannot be skipped. They can't be bolted on later.

So if not with a keen eye toward marketing, where do we properly begin our pursuit of a perennial seller? As my mentor Robert Greene put it, "It starts by wanting to *create a classic.*" Phil Libin, the cofounder of Evernote, has a quote I like to share with clients: "People [who are] thinking about things other than making the best product never make the best product." We're not just talking about making something that is the best for the hell of it. As legendary investor and Y Combinator founder Paul Graham explains, "The best way to increase a startup's growth rate is to make the product so good people recommend it to their friends."

Clearly that doesn't just *happen.* Instead, it must be the highest priority of the creators—they must see this as their calling. They must study the classic work in their fields, emulate the masters and the greats and what made their work last. Timelessness must be their highest priority. They have to learn to ignore distractions. Above all, they have to want to produce meaningful work—which, I can say from experience, is often not the goal of people in the creative space.

The fact is, many people approach their work with polluted intentions. They want the benefits of creative expression, but they desire it without any of the difficulty involved. They want the magic without learning the techniques and the formula. When we look to great works of history as our example, we see one thing: that powerful work is a struggle and that it requires great sacrifice.

The desire for lasting greatness makes the struggle survivable, the sacrifice worth it.

Ideas Are Not Enough

The actress, writer, and comedian Sarah Silverman is often approached by aspiring writers asking for career advice. "I want to be a writer," they tell her. Her response isn't to encourage them or tell them how great they are or to ask to see their work. Silverman doesn't say "You can do it!" or "How can I help?" Instead, she's blunt. "Well, write!" she says. "*Writers write.* You don't wait to get hired on something to write."

Imagine how many people indulge similar fantasies every year: "I should start a company." "I have a great idea for a movie." "I would love to write that book one day." "If I tried hard enough, I could be _____." How many of those people do you think actually go through with building the company, releasing the movie, publishing the book, or becoming whatever it is they claim they could become?

Sadly, almost none.

While many dream perennial-selling dreams, they think that the wanting—instead of the work—is what matters. An aspiring creator once wrote to the filmmaker Casey Neistat about whether he could pitch him about an idea he had. Casey's response was swift and brutally honest: "I don't want to hear your *idea*," he said. "The idea is the easy part."

Neistat was expressing a truth every creator learns, one that is all the more essential in an online world where things can be shared with the click of a button: *Ideas are cheap.* Anyone can have one. There are millions of notebooks and Evernote folders packed with ideas, floating out there in the digital ether or languishing on dusty bookshelves. The difference between a great work and an *idea* for a great work is all the sweat, time, effort, and agony that go into engaging that idea and turning it into something real. That difference is not trivial. If great work were easy to produce, a lot more people would do it.

If you are trying to make something great, *you* must do the making: That work cannot be outsourced to someone else. You can't hire your friends to do it for you. There is no firm that can produce a timeless work of art on your behalf for a flat fee. It's not about finding the right partner, the right investor, the right patron—not yet anyway. Collaboration is essential, but if this is your project, the hard work will fall on you. There is just no way around it.

In my work with authors, I've met with no shortage of smart, accomplished people who, I've realized, don't actually want to write a book despite what they say. They want to *have* a book. We find these types in every industry. We should pity them—because they'll never get what their ego craves so desperately.

I've also learned that wanting to be able to call yourself an author, musician, filmmaker, or entrepreneur is not sufficient fuel to create great work. Especially in a world where it's easier than ever before to call yourself these things—on your social media profiles, on the business cards you order online that show up the next day, on the legal paperwork for an LLC you can draw up online at the cost of a few dollars.

"Lots of people," as the poet and artist Austin Kleon puts it, "want to be the noun without doing the verb." To make something great, what's required is *need*. As in, *I need to do this. I have to. I can't not.*

Why Create?

A lot of people want to play pro ball; few do. It's safe to say that thinking "It'd be fun" is not the critical difference between those who make it and those who don't. The hard part is not the dream or the idea; it's the doing. It is the driving *need* that determines one's chances. You must have a reason—a *purpose*—for why you want the outcome and why you're willing to do the work to get it. That purpose can be almost anything, but it has to be there.

Here are some good ones: Because there is a truth that has gone unsaid for too long. Because you've burned the bridges behind you. Because your family depends on it. Because the world will be better for it. Because the old way is broken. Because it's a once-in-a-lifetime moment. Because it will help a lot of people. Because you want to capture something meaningful. Because the excitement you feel cannot be contained.

These are the states of being that create great works of art—not passing or partial interest—and these are the states you should be seeking out. A desire to impress your friends, or because you think it would be interesting, or because all you care about is quick money—well, that will not be remotely enough.

To create something is a daring, beautiful act. The architect, the author, the artist—all are building something where nothing was before. To try to create something even better than anyone has ever done it before is even bolder. Sitting down at the computer or with a notepad and committing to pour yourself onto it is a scary proposition. But anyone who has done it can tell you that the process is also exhilarating.

It's exhilarating because you are giving something to the world. You are connecting with other people. You are solving a problem for other people. Feeling the work leave your fingertips . . . and then seeing it taken in through someone else's. Expressing some truth that others have been afraid to articulate—in any form. Capturing some experience and preserving it for posterity. It's the ability to remake the planet, to alter the course of history, to escape death, to enter the minds of other people.

There's a reason that so many artists persist through insuperable obstacles—even the starving ones—to do their work. Because it's one of the greatest and most rewarding pursuits in the world.

It also matters. It can make a difference. It can change people. Sure, it can make a lot of money too. It can even make you famous. But these last two benefits are secondary.

The question is: Why are *you* creating? Why are you putting pen to paper and subjecting yourself to all the difficulties you will certainly face along the way? What is your motivation? Because the answers will determine how likely you are to be successful.

This is not a question of "purity." It's simple. Compare two creators: one who cares less about what he's making and more about what it can do for him (make money), and another who, upon sitting down, says, "This is my life's work" or "This is what I was put on this planet to make." Who would you bet on?

Every project must begin with the right intent. It might also need luck and timing and a thousand other things, but the right intent is nonnegotiable—and, thankfully, intent is very much in your control.

What Will You Sacrifice?

George Orwell, author of the classics *1984* and *Animal Farm*, warned prospective writers of the hazards of the profession in his essay "Why I Write." He wrote, "Writing a book is a horrible, exhausting struggle, like a long bout with some painful illness.

One would never undertake such a thing if one were not driven on by some demon whom one can neither resist nor understand."*

Driven on by some demon. Consider that, and then consider the stories you always hear of writers walling themselves off from their friends, families, pretty much anyone and anything that could be a distraction from the work itself. Picture George Lucas literally ripping out his own hair as he struggled to complete the first draft of *Star Wars.* Consider stories of struggling artists who give up everything—even steady meals—for their work. Elon Musk has compared starting a company to "eating glass and staring into the abyss of death." Hunter S. Thompson once said that "the music business is a cruel and shallow money trench, a long plastic hallway where thieves and pimps run free and good men die like dogs." And then he quipped, "There's also a negative side." He could have been talking about any creative industry, just as the actor and director Warren Beatty could have been talking about the feeling of starting a new business or the incubation period of a new book when he used the metaphor of vomiting to describe the filmmaking process: "I don't like vomiting," he said. "But there is a time when you say, 'I'll feel better if I finally throw up.'" If any of that sounds extreme then this probably isn't the journey for you.

These industries are vicious precisely because so many people want to be in them. Their ranks are filled not just with those great creators who are actually doing the hard work, but with legions more who will do literally anything to avoid that work while maintaining their positions (or illusions) of power. Together, they form a suffocating gauntlet that swallows up the many who enter naively

---

* John McPhee put it a little less dramatically: "Write on subjects in which you have enough interest on your own to see you through all the stops, starts, hesitations, and other impediments along the way."

or with all sorts of entitled ideas about how important they are to an industry that is, at best, utterly indifferent to their dreams.

At a book signing I gave a while back, a little girl got up and asked what it took to become a writer. There, exhausted at the end of a two-year sprint to create that book, I couldn't think of a pleasant, bite-size piece of encouragement. All I could think about was what had gone into the book (in short, everything I had) and what I had risked to write it (relationships mostly, but also the gamble to make something new and different that could easily fail). So that's what I told her. I said that to become a writer takes *everything* you have. I quoted that Orwell line too. "You should only be a writer," I said, "if you can't *not* be a writer." Afterward, my wife told me that I'd probably scared the kid. If I did, I'm not exactly sorry about it. Because once you get past the lack of saccharine encouragement, there is real inspiration in the more honest explanations of what it takes to make it.

Think of the walk-on football player struggling through summer two-a-days to get his shot at making the team. Think of the writer working into the night well after everyone in the house has gone to sleep because it's the only quiet time she gets. Think of the artist probing the darkest periods of her life. Think of the musician playing another gig at a venue that will likely stiff him, just to make a few new fans. Think of the stand-up comedian bombing onstage but pushing through it because she knows this is part of the process—because she knows she's getting a little better each time.

Whether these are clichés or inspiring images, there is very real pain involved either way. It's easy to talk about them, harder to *do* them. To actually give something up in the pursuit of your work is not only necessary but rewarding.

From sacrifice comes meaning. From struggle comes purpose. If you're to create something powerful and important, you must at the very least be driven by an equally powerful inner force. If there is anything to romanticize about art, it's the struggle and the dedication required to get it right—and the motivating force that makes it all possible.

In the course of creating your work, you are going to be forced to ask yourself: What am I willing to sacrifice in order to do it? Will I give up X, Y, Z? A willingness to trade off something—time, comfort, easy money, recognition—lies at the heart of every great work. Sometimes more, sometimes less, but always a significant sacrifice that *needs* to happen. If it didn't, everyone would do it.

It's a Marathon, Not a Sprint

Anyone who has run the gauntlet and produced a great product— or even just seen an average one all the way through—knows it's a grueling process. You wake up for weeks, months, or years on end and yet at the end of each working day you are essentially no closer to finishing than you were when you started. Consider the construction on La Sagrada Família in Barcelona, which broke ground in 1882 yet whose completion is slated for 2026—the hundred-year anniversary of the architect's death. The months and years and decades fall away. The Sistine Chapel took four years just to paint; the planning and the building took even longer. Matthew Weiner mused on the idea for *Mad Men* for years after first writing it down. Even finishing the first episode was not the end—or even the halfway point—because no one wanted the show. He called the show his mistress and carried it with him in a bag for years as he worked on other projects, watching it get critiqued and rejected time and again. From the time he started until production on the pilot began some seven long years later, very little visible progress occurred along the way (it was another year after that before he was able to film the second episode). Eventually there were immense rewards for his patience, but let's not forget that even the momentous moment when Weiner got the green light to finally make his beloved show it was simply the *beginning* of seven more arduous years of writing, directing, and filming. Art is the kind of marathon where you cross the finish line and instead of getting a medal placed around your neck, the volunteers roughly grab you by the shoulders and walk you over to the starting line of another marathon.

This is why I asked you about your motivation. This is why intent has such a large impact on your ability to persevere and survive. Because you will be tested. Not once, but repeatedly.

There is inevitably a crisis and a low point in every creative work. We all run smack into what author and marketer Seth Godin calls "the Dip." The existential crisis where we'll have to ask ourselves: Is this even worth it anymore? And it won't be the desire to get rich or famous that drives us out of that valley of despair—it will need to be something deeper and more meaningful.

The filmmaker James Cameron wrote the treatment for *Avatar* in 1994. He was supposed to film it after the completion of *Titanic* in 1997, but he couldn't get started, because the filmmaking technology hadn't caught up to his vision for the project. He did a number of tests using various technologies and filmmaking techniques, but none of them was quite right. He could have thrown up his hands and quit and moved on to one of the dozen other projects on his desk ready to go. But he couldn't do that. Instead, he spent the next several years helping *invent the technology he needed*. Once it met his standards, he then spent the next four years actually making the movie, which was released in December 2009. Cameron revolutionized 3D motion-capture filmmaking, and *Avatar* went on to capture the all-time worldwide box office record by more than half a billion dollars over the second-place film—*Titanic*—which was also his! Cameron is one of the greatest creative minds of his or any generation. Just imagine all the struggles he endured and the opportunities he sacrificed in that fifteen-year window to make *Avatar*.

If you're not sure you have that kind of drive, or if this all sounds unpleasant (granted, to a degree it is), then it might make sense for you to just quit right now. You'll be glad you did. There's no shame in it. Zappos and Amazon offer to pay employees to walk away from their job at the end of a ninety-day trial period. They encourage them to take a onetime payout of $5,000. Why? Because not everyone is right for the job—and it's better to realize that sooner than later.

Great Things Are Timeless and Take Time

On his third album, Drake rapped:

> *I'm tired of hearin' 'bout who you checkin' for now*
> *Just give it time, we'll see who's still around a decade from now*

He was throwing down the same gauntlet as Cyril Connolly in a hits-based "What's hot right now?" industry. Many musicians care about being popular—a lot of them about getting rich and living the rock star life *now*—with little thought as to what will hold up over time.

If making money is *all* you care about, and making it sooner is preferable to later, then a perennial seller is not the path for you. There are better, faster ways to make a profit: work on commission somewhere, start another fusion restaurant, get a job on Wall Street, open a marijuana dispensary. Creating something that lives—that can change the world and continue doing so for decades—requires not just a reverence for the craft and a respect for the medium, but real patience for the process itself.

By *patience*, I'm not referring just to the amount of time that creation will take, but also the long view with which you evaluate your own work. And the long view can be *really* long. Consider all the pieces of art derided and disregarded in their own time, only to be deemed masterworks decades later. Think of the creators whose work was called ludicrous, only to set the standard for a field or spark a new cultural moment.

Two of the most essential principles in the famous "Toyota Way"—the internal philosophy that has guided the Japanese car company for decades—explicitly extol the virtues of taking a long-term view and respecting process. Understanding that systems and processes are important and that decisions must be made with the long view in mind played a role in creating perennial sellers like the Corolla and the Camry. They are principles that everyone in the company—from the CEO to the marketing department to the workers on the assembly lines—must live by every single day.

The same is true for our work. Even if it isn't designed to last quite that long or on such an international scale.

Alexander Hamilton, one of America's founding fathers, produced hundreds of thousands of words over the course of his short five decades on this earth, much of them intended to defend the institutions he and the other founders were creating at the time. As his biographer Ron Chernow observes, it's rather shocking to realize that almost all his work was "journalism"—essentially responses to current events. But his "topical writing has endured"—works like *The Federalist Papers* and George Washington's farewell address (mostly penned by Hamilton)—"because *he plumbed the timeless principles behind contemporary events*" (emphasis mine).

If you've ever caught yourself in some peculiar situation in modern life and then told your friend "It's like that episode of *Seinfeld* where George . . ." or "It's like that one where Kramer goes . . ." or used the phrase "double dip" or accused someone of "regifting" or of being a "close talker," you've experienced some version of this. Written with a stand-up comic's eye, *Seinfeld* has transcended the era it was produced in primarily because, like many classics, it focused on what was timeless about timely events. *Friends*, a contemporary show with *Seinfeld*, focused instead on its attractive and increasingly famous characters at the expense of those themes and so, despite titling each of its episodes "The One Where . . . ," very few people ever actually reference the show in that way. Obviously both shows were successful—incredibly so—but one is a perennial success and the other is a receding cultural memory.*

It's better to do as Hamilton did, as Seinfeld did, and as Jeff Bezos, the founder of Amazon, reminds his employees: "Focus on the things that don't change."

You can't make something that lasts if it's based on things, on individual parts that themselves won't last, or if it's driven by an amateur's impatience. The creative process will require not only time and work, but also the long view. It doesn't matter what the deadlines are or who is breathing down your neck—in a year, will the extra two days you spent seem excessive? In ten years, will spending ten extra days, or even ten weeks, seem like a long time?

When working on my first book, I fought with the publisher over the release date. They wanted me to take my time. Since the

---

* Related, but I like this question: Can you remember a single line from the movie *Avatar*? As the highest-grossing movie of all time, it clearly has its merits and many people call it a favorite, but isn't it interesting how we've completely forgotten it? Could a better script or better dialogue have made the movie even *more* of a cultural hit?

book addressed contemporary issues, I believed I had only this tiny little window to hit to finish and release the book, and if I didn't, I'd miss my chance. Not that I'd have fewer readers, but that if I didn't get this thing out *right now*, I'd have *zero* readers. I felt this sincerely. Of course, this was ridiculous, the naiveté of a first-time author. To my surprise, the revised paperback edition of my exposé of the online media system, published more than three years after I'd first conceived of the idea, not only outsold the original hardcover, it's still selling today.

A few years later, I was reading a work by the great writer Stefan Zweig. In it, he recounts a similar youthful conversation with an older and wiser friend. The friend was encouraging him to travel, believing that the experience would help broaden and deepen Zweig's writing. Like me, Zweig believed he had to write right now and that he didn't have the time to wait—he was feeling the urgency of a first-time writer too. "Literature is a wonderful profession," the friend explained patiently, "because haste is no part of it. Whether a really good book is finished a year earlier or a year later makes no difference."

Art can't be hurried. It must be allowed to take its course. It must be given its space—and can't be rushed or checked off a to-do list on the way to something else.

The old idea that "if it's worth doing, it's worth doing right" is at the core of great businesses. It certainly makes things a bit more intimidating, but necessarily so if lasting greatness is your intention. As Larry Page, the cofounder of Google, explained, "Even if you fail at your ambitious thing, it's very hard to fail completely. That's the thing people don't get."

Short Term vs. Long Term

You know who was rushed? Most of the people who started "businesses" right before the first dot-com bust, or apps for Myspace pages. Or Groupon clones. Or QR codes. Or gourmet cupcakes. Think of the people who rushed to be the first to use Google Glass or Google Plus.

At the time, these ideas seemed irresistibly urgent. Their ambition, their timeline—both were about instantaneousness. The industries were growing like a weed. Investors and publishers and customers were lining up to throw money at them. The media was churning out stories about them. They were rocket ships, and it was a race to jump on and ride the growth. Peter Thiel, the founder of PayPal and the first investor in Facebook, warns that these are precisely the opportunities to avoid. First off, there's too much competition. Second, the hype obscures whether there is the realistic long-term potential we've been pursuing in this book. "If you focus on near-term growth above everything else," he has written, "you miss the most important question you should be asking: Will this business still be around a decade from now?" (See, ten years is a theme.)

Throughout the history of business, people have spotted trends and rushed into business to capitalize on them. Some succeeded. More were rushed right back *out* of business when tastes changed. The first and most essential step in the creation of a perennial business or project for us, then, is to avoid making that mistake.

There's a certain immediacy and availability bias inherent in the decisions that many creators make—it seems right *now*—but time is rarely kind to those choices, even if they do make money in the short term. I've heard people say, "Oh, this project is just a business card for me." I guess I get the logic, but who wants a business card with an expiration date?*

The risk for any creator is over-accounting for what's happening right in front of them. A musician, for instance, can be distracted by what happens to be on the radio at a given moment. A filmmaker might justify a decision to use a certain type of color palette or choose a certain actor because it's a trend very much of the moment. A startup might attempt to solve a problem that's bothering people *right* now, assuming that this will always be true. In the short term, this makes sense—radio is a good barometer for what music fans are interested in, your peers might be on the cutting edge of something important, the startup might be right with its prediction. But what if this moment in time is an aberration? What if trends and tides shift? What if, by the time you capitalize on it, it's already over? A truly successful band, or filmmaker, or entrepreneur—one whose career lasts decades—must think bigger and more long term than that.

Take the *Star Wars* franchise. In one sense, the films were undoubtedly futuristic and took advantage of then cutting-edge special effects. This was a big part of their appeal, in fact. George Lucas has also acknowledged that his initial conception of the movie was for a modern take on the *Flash Gordon* franchise, and he went as far as trying to buy the rights. He also borrowed heavily from the Japanese movie *The Hidden Fortress* for the bickering relationship between R2D2 and C3PO. Yet for all these contemporary influences, Lucas's most profound source material was the work of a then relatively obscure mythologist named Joseph

---

* I've also heard projects analogized as college degrees. As in, "Writing a book is the new college degree." Sure, but if the book is mediocre, what does that say? If you just paid someone to do it all for you, that's like graduating from a for-profit diploma mill. Why bother?

Campbell and his concept of a "hero's journey." Despite the trendy special effects, the story of Luke Skywalker is rooted in the same epic principles of Gilgamesh, of Homer, even the story of Jesus Christ. Lucas has referred to Campbell as "my Yoda" for the way he helped him tell "an old myth in a new way." When you think about it, it's those epic themes of humanity that are left when the newness of the special effects falls away. Why else would fifteen-year-olds—who weren't even born when the *second* set of three movies was made, let alone the original trilogy—still be wowed by these films?

This idea of going back to the core of our shared humanity is a commonality in masterpieces like *Star Wars* as well as in the music of everyone from Johnny Cash to Black Sabbath and the Red Hot Chili Peppers. Rick Rubin, the record producer who has worked with all of those musicians, urges his artists not to think about what's currently on the airwaves. "If you listen to the greatest music ever made, that would be a better way," he says, "to find your own voice to matter today than listening to what's on the radio and thinking: 'I want to compete with this.' It's stepping back and looking at a bigger picture than what's going on at the moment." He also urges them not to constrain themselves simply to their medium for inspiration—you might be better off drawing inspiration from the world's greatest museums than, say, finding it in the current *Billboard* charts.

Thinking big picture—even just trying to envision the world ten years from now—is as exhilarating as it is terrifying. In 2010, Andrew Meieran, a real estate investor, movie producer, and restaurant impresario, bought the then seventy-five-year-old Clifton's Cafeteria in downtown Los Angeles and spent $10 million renovating and expanding it. Why? There were certainly easier projects he could have tackled. He could have opened a sushi restaurant or turned the building into office space. Those things might have been successful, but they might have also failed and disappeared without a trace. Which is why he decided to do something very different. He knew that there was something special about a place that had been in business since 1935 and had endured through so much, unusual decor and all.

As he described it to me when I asked, "One of the things that also drew me to Clifton's was its sense of timelessness. It's difficult to identify when and where it exists. Is it 1930s LA? A forest grove in Northern California? A lodge in the mountains? A hut in the South Pacific? It could be anywhere, anytime. And with that it becomes timeless. It cannot be identified with an era, a trend, or a style. It is so many things that it is constantly in and out of fashion!"

Surely this attitude helped him when the renovations took far longer and cost much more than expected. It was also what created a chance not only to make a lot of money, but to last for another century or more. A chance that most other people missed or could not believe.

The designer Joey Roth—responsible for the iconic Sorapot teapot and a series of high-end ceramic speakers found in the household of every true audiophile—has created an aesthetic around a similar idea: "I see designers and companies whose work represents a disposable, ironic, trend-driven view of product design as my ideological enemies. . . . My desire to design objects that represent a more thoughtful, sustainable view grew partially from the ironic, anti-design trend I encountered as I was getting into design."

It's better to play the longer game. Leave behind the hype and ephemeral infatuations for the time capsule and the one-hit wonders.

Doing so is not simple, however. It can mean tough choices, saying no when everyone wants you to say yes—sometimes even the people closest to you who are counting on you. It will mean going back to the drawing board and tossing out progress. Frank Darabont, the director and writer of *The Shawshank Redemption*, was offered $2.5 million to sell the rights so that Harrison Ford and Tom Cruise could be cast as the stars. He turned it down because he felt this was his "chance to do something really great" with his screenplay and the actors of his choosing. He turned out to be right, but knowing that wouldn't have made the choice any easier at the time. Your choices will be hard too—prepare for it.

Creativity Is Not a Divine Act. It Is Not a Lightning Strike.

While creativity can seem like magic, like every magic trick there is a method behind it. A timeless creation will not simply appear. No matter how much we'd like to believe otherwise, history does not bear out the idea of inspiration flowing unheeded from the muses. Any claims otherwise—as you find out when you actually do the research—turn out to be apocryphal, exaggerated, or just flat-out wrong. Are there some exceptions? Sure, *Rocky* was supposedly written by Sylvester Stallone in three and a half days, but this is the kind of exception that proves the rule. Very few great things were ever created at a hackathon.

Yet it's tempting to think that great work appears ex nihilo. That it simply emerges, in full form, from divine sources. As Hemingway supposedly said, "There is nothing to writing. All you do is sit down at a typewriter and bleed."

This is a wonderful, seductive line as we consider sitting

down at our own proverbial typewriters. The problem is that it is preposterous and *untrue*. It is directly contradicted by Hemingway's own meticulously edited, often handwritten manuscript pages. The John F. Kennedy Presidential Library has some forty-seven alternative endings for Hemingway's *A Farewell to Arms*. He rewrote the first part of the book, by his own count, more than *fifty* times. He wrote all of them, trying them like pieces of a puzzle until one finally fit.

Young aspiring writers like to point to Jack Kerouac, who supposedly wrote *On the Road* in a three-week drug-fueled blitz. What they leave out is the *six years* he spent editing and refining it until it was finally ready. As one Kerouac scholar told NPR on the book's fiftieth anniversary, "Kerouac cultivated this myth that he was this spontaneous prose man, and that everything that he ever put down was never changed, and that's not true. He was really a supreme craftsman, and devoted to writing and the writing process." *

A writer has to be to get it right—getting to five times Cyril Connolly's daunting benchmark is no easy task. Fifty years? A half century—that's longer than people used to live. To do this requires being more than a stationary lightning rod. We must be active. We must work creation into existence.

Indeed, many studies have confirmed that creativity isn't like a lightning strike. A creative work usually starts with an idea that seems to have potential and then evolves with work and interaction into something more. I asked Scott Barry Kaufman, a leading psychologist at the University of Pennsylvania and an expert on creativity, about how ideas happen.

---

* By the way, when it launched, the book was lauded by critics as being *"beautifully executed"* and hit the bestseller lists.

"Insights rarely occur fully baked," he explained. "The creative process is often nonlinear, with many detours along the way that inform the final product. The creator often starts with a hazy intuition of where he or she is going, but breakthrough innovations rarely resemble the seed idea or vision. This is because creative ideas, by their very nature, evolve over time, reflecting the colliding of seemingly disparate ideas. The best we can do is sit down and create something, anything, and let the process organically unfold. Tolerating ambiguity, frustration, and changes in the grand plan and being open to new experiences are essential to creative work. Indeed, they are what makes creativity work."

What the poet John Keats called "negative capability"—the holding of multiple contradictory ideas in your head at the same time—is an essential phase of creativity: the part where your mind is a whirl of ideas. You have to be able to tolerate this and then refine your idea like mad until it gets better.

If there is any magic in creative expression, it's how small, even silly ideas can become big, important, awe-inspiring works if a person invests enough time in them. How within seemingly ordinary people there can exist depths of wisdom, beauty, and insight—and that if they put in the work to plumb those deep depths, they might reap incredible rewards.

There is a reason that many artists have trouble looking back at their own work. They say it feels foreign to them when they do. The reason is that it *is* foreign—or at least, foreign to their basic consciousness. They have trouble even seeing where it came from, even as it touches a raw and vulnerable part of them.

The answer, of course, is that it was created by the process. It was created piece by piece.

The Drawdown Period

To wrestle with all these conflicting, difficult ideas that go into creating, you often need real silence. Meditative isolation, where you sit and wrestle with your project. The gangster Frank Lucas called this "backtracking." He'd lock himself in a room, pull the blinds, and tune everything out. He'd look forward and inward and outward and just think. That was where he finalized what became known as the Cadaver Connection—an operation importing heroin directly from Southeast Asia in imitation coffins smuggled onto U.S. Army jets, which cost a tenth of other methods. On the other end of the creative spectrum, the brilliant military strategist John Boyd utilized what he called "drawdown periods." After a one a.m. breakthrough, he'd spend weeks just looking at an idea, testing whether others had already come up with it, identifying possible problems with it. Only after this period ended would he begin the real work on the project.

In the way that a good wine must be aged, or that we let meat marinate for hours in spices and sauce, an idea must be given space to develop. Rushing into things eliminates that space. Another reason for the drawdown period is simply to prepare for the mammoth nature of the task ahead. A book takes months or years of writing. Movie productions may take longer. Scientific discoveries might take decades to properly articulate. This is not a process we ought to plunge into unknowingly. Just as we take a big breath before we dive underwater, we need to grab some air before we bury ourselves in a creative pursuit.

For one of my books, I gave myself a January 1 start date for the writing. Two months before, in November, I entered my drawdown period. No more reading or rereading. Just thinking. Long walks. Resting. Preparing. I wrapped up the business that I needed to get off my plate. Excited as I was, I couldn't conceive of what the structure of the book would look like. I just wasn't sure that I was ready. I was nervous.

Then one night at the end of December, I had a dream. It was set in the movie *Interstellar*. Everything felt exactly like the previews of that movie. An earth that had begun to fall apart. A crisis was brewing. I was selected as an astronaut. I said good-bye to my children (which I didn't yet have). I put on my helmet. I walked to my spaceship. As I arrived, I found that the spaceship wasn't being launched out of the atmosphere. In the way that things can make sense only inside a dream, this rocket was going to be launched into the depths of the earth.

I have the journal entry I wrote the next morning detailing this strange dream. It's dated December 19—just a few days before I was scheduled to start writing. My subconscious was telling me that I was ready. That it was time to end the drawdown. The dream marked the day that I had to truly embark on the project with everything I had.

Test Early, Test Often

Understand, the book didn't become a reality because I'd been given the gift of clarity from my subconscious. On the contrary, that was just when the real work began. The book that I thought was going to be about the topic of humility didn't survive my attempt to write even one chapter. Honestly, it had trouble surviving anything much longer than dinner conversations with friends.

Thankfully, I listened to the feedback from these early attempts, these tests of the material. The message was clear: The idea needed to be taken in a different direction before I could proceed much further. (I pivoted to a book *against* ego instead of writing a defense of humility.)

Such pivots are common. The Pixar movie *Up*, for example, began as a story about "two princes who lived in a floating city on an alien planet." It was only after digging into the idea and joking around that the writers zeroed in on the theme of "escape" and decided that a fun way to do it would be by attaching balloons to a house. Creative people naturally produce false positives. Ideas that they think are good but aren't. Ideas that other people have already had. Mediocre ideas that contain buried within them the seeds of much better ideas.

The key is to catch them early. And the only way to do that is by doing the work at least partly in front of an audience. A book should be an article before it's a book, and a dinner conversation before it's an article. See how things go before going all in.

Seeking out this feedback is essential—but also dangerous. The screenwriter Brian Koppelman has spoken about the diverse reception he got when he and his writing partner David Levien were working on the screenplay for their first movie, *Rounders*. One person would tell them it was overwritten. The next would tell them it was underwritten. Someone would tell them it was amazing. Someone else would tell them it was terrible.

Whether you're shopping a mostly formed draft, as they were, or you're just brainstorming ideas with potential backers or friends, getting mixed messages is almost a certainty in the creative process. These conflicting, contradictory notes can be simultaneously ego-boosting or soul-crushing if you're not careful. The proper approach is to have a clear idea of what you're trying to accomplish, so you can parse the constructive criticism you need from the notes you need to ignore. (In Brian's case, it was supposed to be overwritten—the movie was designed to be incredibly quotable. In my case, I was testing my different approaches and found that the one I had embarked on wasn't working.)

In the startup world, founders have a special version of that process, called Minimum Viable Product, which involves starting with a small idea and then testing it relentlessly with small focus groups until it becomes the best version of itself (or, conversely, it gets killed because it doesn't actually have that much potential). The approach has some benefits in other domains too. If you're a chef, it might not be an amazing idea to pour your life savings into your first restaurant venture when you can start a food truck or a pop-up shop first. Don't spend months building a website—start with a landing page, or rely on free social media platforms.

Los Angeles–based Kogi Korean BBQ is credited with starting the food truck craze between 2008 and 2009. In the beginning, they used Twitter exclusively to announce where around LA they'd be parked each day. It was a brilliant and efficient strategy. Over time, as they built on their success and made incremental changes to the menu and the business, Kogi expanded to five trucks. They didn't open their first brick-and-mortar restaurant until 2016.

Creating is often a solitary experience. Yet work made entirely in isolation is usually doomed to remain lonely.

This is good news. It means that your perennial seller does not have to be birthed in some single episode of genius. Instead, it can be made piece by piece—or, as Anne Lamott put it in her meditation on writing, "bird by bird." You don't have to be a genius to make genius—you just have to have small moments of brilliance and edit out the boring stuff.

How we put this into practice is simple: Ask questions. How can I give people a sample of what I'm thinking? How does the idea resonate in conversation? What does an online audience think of it? What does a poll of your friends reveal? These might seem like small questions in the face of a big task like creating a classic work that lasts—but classics are built by thousands of small acts. And thinking about them in that way allows you to make progress.

In asking questions and soliciting input, you're not letting other people determine what you work on. But by thinking this way you substantially reduce the fantastically inhuman pressure to be great simply by epiphany or a visit from the muses. Instead, it's about finding the germ of a good idea and then *making it* a great product through feedback and hard work. Forget going off into some cave.

Focusing on smaller, progressive parts of the work also eliminates the tendency to sit on your ass and dream indefinitely. There is no question that planning is really important, *but* it's seductive to get lost in that planning—to hope that the perfect project simply floats your way instead of deciding that it's on you to make it.

As Robert Evans, the movie producer behind films like *Love Story* and *The Godfather*, put it, "Getting into action generates inspiration. Don't cop out waiting for inspiration to get you back into action. It won't!"

The Question Almost No One Asks

In my library I have a little book called *Worms Eat My Garbage* by Mary Appelhof. Unless you're a permaculture nerd, there's no reason you'd have heard of this book. That's the whole point—the book is only for permaculture nerds, or at least aspiring ones. While most people haven't heard of the book, this indie-published engine-that-could has gone on to sell some 165,000 copies (more than most books will ever sell) and is still in print some thirty-five years after its initial publication. It's on its second expanded and revised edition—the first came fifteen years after initial release, the second twenty years after that. Not only is *Worms Eat My Garbage* the definitive text in a small but passionate space, it's dominating the kind of niche that's probably always going to exist (unless society suddenly stops producing garbage).

Dialing in this kind of domain dominance doesn't happen accidentally. An audience isn't a target that you happen to bump into; instead, it must be explicitly scoped and sighted in. It must be *chosen*. There is a small publisher whose slogan is "Find your niche and scratch it!" I suspect if Mary Appelhof knew about this publisher when she wrote her book in 1982, it might have been the first place she went with her manuscript.

Successfully finding and "scratching" a niche requires asking and answering a question that very few creators seem to do: *Who is this thing for?*

Instead, many creators want to be for everyone . . . and as a result end up being for no one.

Picking a lane isn't limiting. It's the first act of empowerment we take as a creator. Recently Charlie Rose asked Lin-Manuel Miranda, creator of the blockbuster musical *Hamilton*, what set him apart from some of the smarter, more talented kids he had gone to school with. Miranda answered: " 'Cause I picked a lane and I started running ahead of everybody else . . . I was like, 'All right, THIS.' "

For any project, you must know what you are doing—and what you are *not* doing. You must also know who you are doing it for—and who you are *not* doing it for—to be able to say: THIS and for THESE PEOPLE. In some cases, that might be an enormous niche. In Miranda's situation, it's people looking for a very different kind of Broadway show. In Appelhof's situation, it was people looking to get into composting. Regardless of what it is, you have to know. You have to choose. Having this clarity allows you to focus your creative energy in a very narrow, effective way. It allows you to focus that energy on making the right thing for the right people.

You certainly can't expect to scratch an itch you can't identify—or stay in a lane you've yet to define—and it's naive to think that you'll be able to scratch every itch on everyone in the world. Yet this is precisely what most creatives do with their projects from the outset. Paul Graham of startup incubator Y Combinator, which has funded more than a thousand startups, including Dropbox, Airbnb, and Reddit, says that "having no specific user in mind" is one of the eighteen major mistakes that kills startups: "A surprising number of founders seem willing to assume that someone—they're not sure exactly who—will want what they're building. Do the founders want it? No, they're not the target market. Who is? Teenagers. People interested in local events (that one is a perennial tar pit). Or 'business' users. What business users? Gas stations? Movie studios? Defense contractors?"

Let's be clear: You can't afford to wait until *after* it's finished to figure out who what you're making is for. Why? Because too often the answer turns out to be: no one. You have to think about it now. Before you've made it. While you're making it.

The absence of an intended audience is not just a commercial problem. It is an artistic one. The critic Toby Litt could have been talking about all bad art and bad products when he said that "bad writing is almost always a love poem addressed by the self to the self." What audience wants that?

The best way I've found to avoid missing your target—any target—entirely is to identify a proxy from the outset, someone who represents your ideal audience, who you then think about constantly throughout the creative process. Stephen King believes that "every novelist has a single ideal reader" so that at various points in the process he can ask, "What will _____ think about this?" (For him, it's his wife, Tabitha.) Kurt Vonnegut joked that you have to "write to please just one person. If you open a window and make love to the world, so to speak, your story will get pneumonia." John Steinbeck once wrote in a letter to an actor turned writer, "Forget your generalized audience. In the first place, the nameless, faceless audience will scare you to death, and in the second place, unlike the theater, it doesn't exist. In writing, your audience is one single reader. I have found that sometimes it helps to pick out one person—a real person you know, or an imagined person—and write to that one."

If you don't know who you're writing for or who you're making for, how will you know if you're doing it right? How will you know if you've *done* it? You are unlikely to hit a target you haven't aimed for. *Hope* is not helpful here; having something and someone to measure against is.

Avoid this potential miss by articulating and defining the specific audience while you are creating—yet don't make it so specific that the only member of that audience is *you*. You must be able to see them, to empathize with them, to understand and even love them. Not that this audience will be the only thing you have to have in mind as you create (and as you'll see later, having it in mind is no guarantee of reaching it), but it must be in there, rattling around somewhere.

Not Just, "Who For?" Also, "For What?"

As creatives, we can often become consumed with what a certain project means to us personally. We're in love with it, obsessed with it—that's why we're willing to spend so much time on it. Swooning in our own artistic self-satisfaction, our standards include: Is this fulfilling our grand vision? Are we beating out some competitor?

Is it making us look good? How does it fit with our brand and image as fearless artists? This is often just ego in disguise—feasting on our own thoughts because it's easier than thinking about your audience.

It's a dangerous trance that has sent many talented creators down hopeless dead ends.

An editor once told me, "It's not what a book is, it's what a book *does*." Jerry Jenkins, creator of the *Left Behind* series, has said that regardless of *what* we make or *what* we make is *about*, our work must "always be *for the purpose* of something."

It's not that hard to make something *we* want, or something we think is cool or impressive. It's much harder to create something other people not only want, but need. Just as we should ask "Who is this for?" we must also ask "What does this *do*?" A critical test of any product: Does it have a purpose? Does it add value to the world? How will it improve the lives of the people who buy it?

Again, this shouldn't be something you search for after the fact—it should be baked in from day one. Great, successful work rarely starts as a solution in search of a problem. Lasting resonance requires something more than novelty: It needs an earnest person attempting to find a solution to a common problem.* I said something to that effect to Craig Newmark, who founded Craigslist two decades ago (he doesn't run it day to day anymore, but his philosophy has been enough to keep the site focused and effective). He told me that he started Craigslist mostly to reciprocate the exact service that other San Franciscans had done for him—help

---

* A recent study of more than a hundred failed startups determined that "tackling problems that are interesting to solve rather than those that serve a market need was cited as the number one reason for failure in a notable 42% of cases."

him get settled into a new city. "That began a pattern which continues to this day: Talk to people, then do something that meets real needs and wants. Repeat that, forever. People need to socialize, they need a job, and a place to live, and more. The focus is on real needs and wants, not being cool or fancy."

One of the best pieces of advice I've gotten as a creator was from a successful writer who told me that the key to success in nonfiction was that the work should be either "very entertaining" or "extremely practical." Notice they didn't say, "Should be very fulfilling to you personally" or "Should make you look super smart" or "Capitalize on some big trend." Those concerns are either secondary or implied. It's better to be focused on those two timeless use cases of enjoyability or utility.

You want what you're making to *do* something for people, to help them *do* something—and have *that* be why they will talk about it and tell other people about it. That kind of purpose is not something that can be bolted on by an expert marketer or publicist down the road. Instead, it must be integrated into the creative process from the beginning (after all, this is the best marketing there is). Even if the purpose is simply that it provides a few minutes of satisfying entertainment, to ask a probing question or to speak to some part of the human experience. Even a pop song has a purpose. The ones that don't? They don't last—not longer than their fifteen minutes, anyway.

The more important and perennial a problem (or, in the case of art, the more clearly it expresses some essential part of the human experience), the better chance the products that address it will be important and perennial as well. As Albert Brooks put it, "The subject of dying and getting old never gets old." The filmmaker Jon Favreau, who created *Swingers* and *Elf* and directed *Iron Man*, has said that he aims to touch upon timeless problems and myths in his work, and that all great filmmakers do as well. "The ones that get the closest to it," he said, "last the longest."

The bigger and more painful the problem you solve, the better its cultural hook, and the more important and more lucrative your attempt to address it can be. Imagine writing about a problem that solves itself or has a firm expiration date. Ask the people who made "solutions" for Y2K how that worked out for them. Instead, the timeless, recurring problems that make us human—those are ambitious problems to tackle. Some examples:

- Delis like Katz's and Langer's—which have been serving customers for close to two hundred years combined—serve as a safe place for Jewish people to reconnect with the food and culture of their people. And due to their unbelievable longevity, the restaurants have been cultural touchstones for everyone else too.
- Pixar movies like *Toy Story* and *Monsters, Inc.* solved a problem shared by parents and kids alike: Kids want to be entertained, and parents don't want to be bored to tears. So the movies skillfully provided something for both—not just for a few fleeting hours, but for a lifetime of watching and rewatching.
- WD-40 solves one of the most timeless problems of all: entropy. Things get rusty and stuck, and WD-40 helps grease things along and gets them going again.
- GoreTex. People get cold and wet and always have. Brands don't have time to invent their own cold-weather linings and waterproofing. For fifty years, they've used GoreTex because it addresses that problem and customers trust it.
- *What to Expect When You're Expecting.* Every day people get pregnant for the first time (and realize they're totally clueless about the entire process), so they turn to this book.

- "Happy Birthday," which has long had one of the most controversial and contested copyrights, is the ultimate example. Before
that song, what were people supposed to do at a birthday party?

The list goes on and on.

So the creator of any project should try to answer some variant
of these questions:

- What does this teach?
- What does this solve?
- How am I entertaining?
- What am I giving?
- What are we offering?
- What are we sharing?

In short: What are these people going to be paying for? If
you don't know—if the answer isn't overwhelming—then keep
thinking.

Bold, Brash, and Brave

I hope it doesn't sound like I am turning the beautiful artistic and
creative process into a reductive, boring mathematical exercise, or
trying to replace inspiration with the scheming tactics of some
Internet marketer who searches for SEO terms. This isn't about
focus-grouping or replacing purpose with coldhearted business
logic. On the contrary, these exercises are designed to help you find
new ground—to let you be creative and for that creativity to actually resonate. The reason to ask the question "What are they paying for?" is not to advocate crass commercialism. It's to push
you—to push you out of your comfort zone until your answer to

that question is "Something new and important" instead of "Something anyone else could have made."

As we know, ideas are cheap. Not only do lots of people have ideas, but you, as a talented, creative person, are going to have lots of ideas. Some of those ideas will be derivative and others will be wildly original. Others may not seem special at first, but with the proper refinement, as you push deeper and deeper, they can become fresh and new and totally unique.

Again, it's not that creativity is magical. It just *appears* to be magic to people who don't understand the trick. In this case, the most important part of the trick is filtering out the seemingly lucrative but ultimately derivative dead ends that you might otherwise have pursued.

An essential part of making perennial, lasting work is making sure that you're pursuing the best of your ideas and that they are ideas that *only you* can have (otherwise, you're dealing with a commodity and not a classic). Not only will this process be more creatively satisfying, it will be better for business. In 2005, business professors W. Chan Kim and Renée Mauborgne described a new concept that they called Blue Ocean Strategy. Instead of battling numerous competitors in a contested "red ocean," their studies revealed that it was far better to seek fresh, uncontested "blue" water.

Cirque du Soleil, Southwest Airlines, Curves, Under Armour, Tesla, and the Nintendo Wii are all clear blue ocean plays. They were new, wildly different from anything else in their industry, and as a result grew rapidly. They were just so inherently exciting and fresh. They broke new ground and then owned it, in some cases for decades before the competition caught up.

As Goethe observed, the most original artworks "are not rated as such because they produce something new" but because they are saying something "as though it had never been said before." They are blue oceans, providing something new or timeless. Pete Carroll, the Super Bowl–winning coach of the Seattle Seahawks, once told me a lesson he learned from the Grateful Dead. The Dead weren't trying to be the *best* at anything, he said; they were trying to be the *only ones doing what they were doing.* Srinivas Rao, a writer and podcaster, put it well: "*Only* is better than *best.*"

Yet far too many people set out to produce something that, if they were really honest with themselves, is only marginally better or different from what already exists. Instead of being bold, brash, or brave, they are derivative, complementary, imitative, banal, or trivial. The problem with this is not only that it's boring, but that it subjects them to endless amounts of competition.

You've probably heard this from fellow creatives when asking them about projects they're working on. They've gone so far down the rabbit hole, they've lost sight of the fact that 90 percent of users are perfectly happy with the dominant player in the space they are trying to occupy, whether it's Facebook or *The Catcher in the Rye.* They can't seem to understand that most customers won't get excited about a moderate improvement—because most people don't even care. I'm always wary of any description that resembles "It's like _____ but with _____." I'm wary of it not only because it's inherently unoriginal, but also because, again, it forces the creators to compete with the very dominant entity they are supposedly improving on.

Being brave and brash is not only more fun creatively, it saves you from going head-to-head with the Facebook (a social network with billions of dollars in revenue) or the *Catcher in the Rye* of your space. It saves you from a costly war of attrition that you will likely lose.

The higher and more exciting standard for every project should force you to ask questions like this:

What sacred cows am I slaying?

What dominant institution am I displacing?

What groups am I disrupting?

What people am I pissing off?

The Nigerian writer Chigozie Obioma has talked about the importance of audaciousness in making something that lasts. "Writers should realize," he said, "that the novels that are remembered, that become monuments, would in fact be those which err on the part of audacious prose, which occasionally allow excess rather than those which package a story—no matter how affecting—in inadequate prose."

With *Born to Run*, Bruce Springsteen said he was trying to make a record that would "grab you by the throat and *insist* that you take that ride, insist that you pay attention." He said he was aspiring to make the "greatest rock record [he'd] ever heard." Brashness, newness, boldness—these attitudes are not at all at odds with perennial sales. In fact, it's an essential part of the equation. Stuff that's boring now is probably going to be boring in twenty years. Stuff that looks, sounds, reads, and performs like everything else in its field today has very little chance of standing out tomorrow. That's exactly what you *don't* want.

Imagine you're Rick Rubin, signed on to produce the first major label album for Slayer, then a notoriously heavy but obscure metal band. The natural impulse for many would be to help the band make something more mainstream, more accessible. But

Rubin knew that would be a bad choice both artistically and commercially. Instead, he helped them create their heaviest album ever—maybe one of the heaviest albums of all time: *Reign in Blood*. As he recounted later, "I didn't want to water down. The idea of watering things down for a mainstream audience, I don't think it applies. People want things that are really passionate. Often the best version is not for everybody. The best art divides the audience. If you put out a record and half the people who hear it absolutely love it and half the people who hear it absolutely hate it, you've done well. Because it is pushing that boundary."

Yes, in the short term, this choice almost certainly cost them some radio play. But when Rubin says that the best art divides the audience, he means that it divides the audience between people who don't like it and people who *really like it*. Ultimately, it was the polarizing approach that turned *Reign in Blood* into a metal classic—an underground album that spent eighteen weeks on the charts and has sold well over two million copies to date.

Erring on the side of audaciousness—trying to grab the customer by the throat—is partly why a lot of the projects we are talking about were wildly controversial and, in some cases, deeply upsetting when they launched. Think of Orson Welles combining fact and fiction in his famous radio broadcast of *The War of the Worlds*—in the moment he was reinventing entertainment and deeply scaring people at the same time. Think of Matisse's *Blue Nude* being burned in effigy in 1913. (Today you can buy a print of it at Walmart.) Think of D. H. Lawrence's novels banned for their obscenity. Think of Truman Capote's *In Cold Blood*, which invented a new genre of nonfiction—people were incensed; was it real or not?! Think of the technology that is subject to protests and reactive legislation—from Airbnb to Uber. Eventually, they become a part of our daily lives, but at first there is something deeply shocking and forceful to them. "Either you're controversial," as the perpetually controversial writer Elizabeth Wurtzel advises creatives, "or nothing at all is happening."

It's interesting to think of how audacious this work is, but also how conventional it is. *Blue Nude* was provocative because of its use of color, of race, of ambiguity. It's not also fifty feet wide and painted with a machine. Orson Welles's broadcast was the length of his normal radio program; Truman Capote didn't decide to publish his book anonymously and without a cover; Airbnb didn't launch as a homesharing service that accepted only cryptocurrency. No, these groundbreaking innovations were unconventional in just a few particular, targeted ways, and that was enough.

The point is that you cannot violate every single convention simultaneously, nor should you do it simply for its own sake. In fact, to be properly controversial—as opposed to incomprehensible—you must have obsessively studied your genre or industry to a degree that you know which boundaries to push and which to respect. There's a reason that shows on Netflix and HBO—even though they don't have commercial breaks—are still roughly thirty or sixty minutes long. In the self-published era, authors can theoretically do whatever they want, yet in most cases they don't. Why? Because not every convention is worth questioning, and, usually, questioning too many at the same time is confusing and overwhelming to the consumer. (They still want their book to seem like a *real* book.)

So we ask ourselves: Why are things the way they are? What practices should be questioned and which should remain sound? This allows us to be both exotic and accessible, shocking but not gratuitous, fresh without sacrificing timelessness.

If you do push boundaries, it's important to understand that not everyone will love it—not right out of the gate, anyway. After publishing my first book, which was incendiary, I received a picture from Ford's head of social media—he'd thrown the book in his trash can, he was so angry about it. One reporter physically accosted me after I gave a talk. I was challenged to a debate by one person in the book; another threatened legal action. It was scary. But it was also exhilarating—and validating.

I've come to realize that these are the tracking signs of a work that lasts. You want to provoke a reaction—it's a sign you're forging ahead. A famous scientist once warned his students not to worry about people stealing their ideas: "If it's original, you will have to ram it down their throats." Not only does that go back to our previous discussion of why mere ideas are not sufficient, but it connects to one of the realities of being provocative and new. Your work may shock people, they might not be willing to accept it right away—but that's also a sign that you've created something fresh and truly original.

Is It the Best You Can Do?

Earlier I mentioned the myth of spontaneous creation. Allow me to return to it, because nothing has so damaged the chances of bringing perennial sellers into this world than that big lie.

Orson Welles said that a movie "must be better to see the second or third time than it is the first time. There must be more in it to see at once than any one person can grasp. It must be so 'meaty,' so full of implications, that everyone will get something out of it." Cyril Connolly said that literature is writing meant to be read twice—everything else is mere journalism. The same goes for great television like *Arrested Development*, where the show is so fast and funny that each rewatching reveals something else. Great books of timeless wisdom offer the same joys. Pick them up and open them at random—something will call out to you and help alleviate your suffering, even if you've already read the book a dozen times.

Our goal here is to make something that people rave about, that becomes part of their lives. The buried insights found in those other great works were not put there on the first pass. Work is unlikely to be layered if it is written in a single stream of consciousness. No. Deep, complex work is built through a relentless, repetitive process of revisitation.

There is always more you can do, more you can add. We talked earlier about the importance of thinking big picture, but we must also think small—as in focusing on the tiniest parts of the process and doing them well. A master is painstakingly obsessed with the details. If you ever peer inside an Apple computer, you'll find they're beautiful on the inside too. The people who design them see the entire product as a work of art—as their masterpiece. They don't cut corners, even on the parts most people will never see.

As one agent I work with put it to me, "Spend three times longer revising your manuscript than you think you need." He's right. It will be the best time you spend almost anywhere in the project. There's a famous bit of advice from Stephen King to "kill your darlings, kill your darlings, even when it breaks your egocentric little scribbler's heart, kill your darlings." Basically, he's talking about the tough decisions that creators must make as they create, as they ruthlessly edit and evolve their creations until they're as good as they can possibly be.

The screenwriting guru and story legend Robert McKee told me that he isn't sure a person can write something great on purpose. But he is certain that we need to do our best on every component part. "I don't think anyone can actually set out consciously to produce a masterpiece," he said. "I think what we do is to tell the best story we can, the best way we can, and produce it in the best way possible, and then see how the world reacts to it." Ignore what other people are doing. Ignore what's going on around you. There is no competition. There is no objective benchmark to hit. There is simply the best that you can do—that's all that matters.

One Last Thing

You might think you already have your classic—your perennial masterpiece. But the truth is, you don't. Not yet, anyway. Not this early in the process. Nobody does. And the people who are especially convinced they do? They especially *don't*. These words of Steven Pressfield in his wonderful book *The War of Art* are a haunting and humbling reminder: "The counterfeit innovator is wildly self-confident. The real one is scared to death."

They're scared because creative work is as terrifying as it is gratifying. You've put a large piece of yourself into this project. What if people don't like it? What if someone tries to force you to change it? Creating was done in private, but soon you'll have to explain and discuss in public. What if that's painful? What if you can't do it justice? This fear isn't comfortable, but it's a good sign. It will make you diligent.

The hunger and drive to create something great, coupled with the sincere belief that *you can do it*, can very quickly trip into delusion and hubris if you're not vigilant. The more nervous and scared you are—the more you feel compelled to go back and improve and tweak because *you're just not ready*—the better it bodes for the project. Because your goal is one that should make any rational person tremble a bit.

Let that feeling guide you. Honor it.

Meanwhile, those who think they can rush their way to that finish line—or have complete confidence they will get there without breaking a sweat—end up disappearing just as quickly. It takes time and effort and sacrifice to make something that lasts.

Part II

POSITIONING

From Polishing to Perfecting to Packaging

The artist seeks contact with his intuitive sense of the gods, but in order to create his work, he cannot stay in this seductive and incorporeal realm. He must return to the material world in order to do his work.

—Patti Smith

In his 1930s novel *Ask the Dust*, John Fante has a scene in which the autobiographical main character sends his manuscript to a publisher. The aspiring author, Arturo Bandini, young and poor, actually requests they send the manuscript back if rejected—because it is his only copy.

As it happens, the publisher doesn't need to send the pages back. Instead, after a long period of silence, they finally respond by answering the young writer's dreams—he gets the call that every creative hopes for, the call that brings us into the big leagues.

There was a knock on my door. I opened the door, and there he stood, a telegraph boy. I signed for the telegram, sat on the bed, and wondered if the wine had finally got the Old Man's heart. The telegram said: your book accepted mailing contract today . . . That was all. I let the paper float to the carpet. I just sat there. Then I got down on the floor and began kissing the telegram. I crawled under the bed and just lay there. I did not need the sunshine anymore. Nor the earth, nor heaven. I just lay there, happy to die. Nothing else could happen to me. My life was over.

A few days later a check and a contract arrive. The book is published a few months after that. He's officially an author. His life of struggle is over. He'd *made* it.

If you have any experience with traditional publishers or record labels or movie studios or even venture capital, this probably sounds impossibly anachronistic or hopelessly naive. Where were all the meetings? Proposals? Pitches? The agents? The lunches? The midnight calls to the editor as the walls feel like they're closing in? The demands for changes and rewrites and "notes" from the suits? The million other bureaucratic and administrative details? You're saying that people used to just mail their stuff in and then it'd show up in stores?

Deep down, we all harbor a fantasy: We do creative work, throw it in the mail—someone else sends us a contract and doesn't bother us again. No one gets to tell us what to do; our art remains pure and untouched. No interference. No pesky concerns about this or that. Someone else handles the stuff we don't care about. We're just "chosen" and then, suddenly, success.

Except that's not how it goes. Not now, not ever. I say that not just because the economics of all these industries have fundamentally changed, but because it didn't work out super well for John Fante either. In real life, *Ask the Dust* was entrusted to the publisher Stackpole and Sons, which didn't have the resources to properly prep and publish Fante's manuscript due to the fact that the company was *in the middle of a legal battle with Adolf Hitler.* The publisher lost—having published *Mein Kampf* without the proper copyright—and Fante, who was totally dependent on them, watched his greatest work simply disappear into the ether because the publisher ran into financial trouble and couldn't market it.

Can you imagine? All your dreams of success ruined by a murderous dictator who managed to reach across the Atlantic and screw with your project via a sloppy publisher that allowed that to happen. Of course, a literal Hitler is rare, but artists' dreams are dashed with cruel regularity. Had Fante's book been better served by his publisher, by his editor, by the author himself, could its fate have turned out differently? I'd like to think so.

In any case, because of poor planning, because of naive hopes, because of overreliance on someone else, this wonderful book never really made it out into the world. It could have been the West Coast *Great Gatsby.* Instead, it was almost entirely forgotten.

The first wake-up call for every aspiring perennial seller must be that there is no publisher or angel investor or producer who can magically handle all the stuff you don't want to handle. Sending in your proverbial manuscript is not the end of the hard work on a project—it's not even the end of the beginning of the amount of work required. There will be no knock on the door, metaphorically or otherwise. Perennial sellers are made by indefatigable artists who, instead of handing off their manuscripts to nonexistent caretakers—"kissing it up to God," to use a Hollywood expression—see every part of the process as their responsibility. They take control of their own fate. Not simply as artists but as *makers* and *managers*.

Halfway to Halfway

Where we are now—a nearly completed screenplay, a startup idea beginning to fully take shape, a product with serious investor interest—is a critical juncture. You might say we are halfway to the halfway point.

What we have done is taken our inner experience or inspiration and made it real. Now it's necessary to take that inner creative experience we captured and polish, refine, and ultimately figure how to best communicate it to the world. The book you wrote to help you deal with your father's death, the song demos you've just finished and are ready to take into the studio, or the clothing line you hope will challenge beauty norms in the fashion industry— these complex personal projects must be examined, polished, and then presented to the world in a way that appeals to the audience. ("A moving exploration of the grieving process that will help readers in their most vulnerable moments" or "Great clothes that will make you look fantastic—*and* we don't exploit or lie in order to sell them to you.") That transition doesn't just happen. The work doesn't go from demo to finished record by itself. And nobody just hands you the perfect title, cover, and artwork.

Audiences can't magically know what is inside something they haven't seen. They have no clue that it will change their lives. You can't be the self-conscious wallflower in the corner, hoping that people will see through the act and just *know* how great you are. Someone is going to have to *tell them*. It has to be obvious!

It's not "promotion" we're talking about here—that comes

later. Instead, prior to release, considerable effort needs to be spent polishing, improving, and, most critically, positioning your project so that it has a real chance of resonating with its intended audience. Even the most delicious dish must be properly plated (and presentation affects the taste—that's a fact). The difference between a nice contemporary hit and a lasting icon is made in these decisions, and this process is not necessarily done quickly. It may be that the editing and refining of a work may take as long as the initial flurry of creation—it could be that the last mile takes longer than all the others put together. It may be that picking the right name for your product or clarifying your goals and expectations into an actionable plan is harder than it was bringing the idea from a nascent thought to physical form.

We have to take this thing that means so much to *us* and make sure that it is primed to mean something to *other people too* for generations to come. That it will stand out among a crowded field of other creators sincerely attempting to do the exact same thing. That it will be the best that it is capable of being and that the audience it is intended for is primed to love it.

And the best person in the world to accomplish this difficult task? You.

You're the CEO

If the first step in the process is coming to terms with the fact that no one is coming to save you—there's no one to take this thing off your hands and champion it the rest of the way home—then the second is realizing that the person who is going to need to step up is *you*.

Many creatives want to be *just the creator,* or only "the idea guy." They like that because it's sexy and because that's what comes easy to us. But I suspect we like it also because we're afraid.

We're afraid of taking full responsibility for everything that comes next. A lot of decisions are going to be made—many of which can sink or make a project—that it'd be nice to have someone else to put it on. If we hand it off to someone else, then we have someone to blame when the project fails.

The studio chose the title. I didn't want to release it in the summer—that was their idea. I wish I could have . . . They shouldn't have . . . Next time I'll . . .

Adults create perennial sellers—and adults take responsibility for themselves. Children expect opportunities to be handed to them; maturity is understanding you have to go out and make them. The competitive landscape for creating something that lasts is not one for the entitled or the half committed. There is so much more competition these days—the ocean is redder than it's ever been. More than four hundred hours of content is uploaded to YouTube every *minute*. Every year, more than 6,000 startups apply to Y Combinator. Ten thousand people get advanced degrees in drama. More than 125,000 people graduate with MBAs each year, and more than 300,000 books are published in the United States. Even with only 5 percent unemployment in the United States, some eight million people are looking for work. Nobody has a reason or the time to give you the star treatment. Nobody wants the hassle of cultivating a diamond in the rough. If you want to be successful, you'd better be cut, polished, set, and sized to fit.

What does that mean? At a very basic level, if you're not amazing in every facet, you're replaceable. To publishers, studios, investors, *and* customers alike.

Seth Godin explains that "being really good is merely the first step. In order to earn word of mouth, you need to make [your product] safe, fun, and worthwhile to overcome the social hurdles to spread the word."

The operative word there is *you*. YOU need to do this. You are the CEO of your work. All the responsibility and leadership falls on you, as the creator—even if you have partners like a publicist, buyer, publisher, or whatever. Just because you have help doesn't mean they're going to take care of everything for you, or that they will arrive at consensus, or that it will all turn out for the best.

In those moments of conflict and confusion, who else but you has the vision for what this thing should be? Who else understands where it fits into your career? Who else will care about the painstaking details and the consistency and integrity and the other little matters that add up to separate the memorable from the mediocre? Who else has the financial interest or the incentives to put in the effort to take this all the way?

To go back to the metaphor of a book, anyone can pick a cover for a book or throw together a safe title, but who can know the best choice for either of those decisions? *Only you.* Anyone can give notes on a script or suggest ideas for improvements to a product. But who can separate the helpful from the harmful? *Only you.* Who else can make the gut call against all advice, or who, when it comes down to it, will stand up for the integrity of the work?

The answer is you and only you.

Find Your "Editor"

Once you understand that this project's chances of success or failure rest entirely on you, you must undertake a paradoxical and difficult task: finding and submitting your work to the feedback of a trusted outside voice (or, in some cases, *voices*).

What is the important thing that writers do when they finish a draft? They hand it to an editor. An *editor*. Not: They send it to some friends for some thoughts. Although they may get great help from friends, it's ultimately the editor with whom writers collaborate. The industry term is illustrative: A writer *submits* a manuscript to an editor.

In the same way, screenwriters *attach* producers with whom they develop a project. Musicians have an *engineer*, and a *producer* finishes an album with them (it's also later *mastered*). Even Michael Jordan played *for* a head coach.

Why? Because when people are close to their own projects or their own talents, they can lose the ability to see objectively. They might think they've taken a project or their talent as far as it can go, and, strictly speaking, given an individual's limitations and inexperience, this may be true. But ultimately, to take a project where it needs to go, you'll need to rely on an editor to help you get there. This is the most counterintuitive part of any creative process—just when you think you're "done," you'll often find you're not even close to being finished.

Here is another famous Hemingway line on writing: "The first draft of anything is shit." Imagine if every author or creator were given carte blanche to make whatever he or she wanted—a world in which no one ever challenged others' work and green-lighted it sight unseen. As appealing as this might seem to creators, the result would be an avalanche of terrible first drafts released as final products. Most of our ideas, upon their initial implementation, turn out to be laughably wrong. Which is why we need help— which is why an important step in Part II of this book is taking the time to revisit what we made in Part I.

In 1957, the young first-time novelist Harper Lee submitted her manuscript to an editor named Tay Hohoff. The editor was receptive but made it clear that, in her opinion, this book would require significant reworking before being published. In Tay's words, the book was "more a series of anecdotes than a fully conceived novel." Presumably, Lee's intention had been to create a full novel, and we can assume she thought she had done so when she delivered the manuscript to her editor. Yet here she was, being told by someone she trusted that she may have failed.

So much in the history of art and culture hinges on moments like this. Faced with soul-crushing feedback or rejection, how does the creator respond? With petulance and anger? With open-mindedness and interest? With obsequiousness and desperation? Or careful consideration that parses the signal from noise? It is the creator's choice at this critical juncture that determines so much— whether the project dies right there, whether it is changed beyond recognition by committee, or whether it is transformed from a decent first attempt into a masterpiece.

Fortunately for all of us, Harper Lee was wise enough to listen. Over the course of several rewrites that took more than two years—essentially an entirely new cast of characters and a new plot, while retaining her unique and essential perspective—Lee created *To Kill a Mockingbird*, one of the great works of American literature.

This process is usually obscured to us—we don't get to listen to Adele's discarded demos and see how what was kept was improved and reimagined. We don't get to see many books "pre-editor," or see how a creator was helped to fully realize his or her true vision. *To Kill a Mockingbird* is a unique case, however. Some fifty-five years later, Lee's original manuscript was published as *Go Set a Watchman*. Despite the initial fanfare, it proved that Lee's editor was right. The book is just not that good—the characters are not fully formed, their attitudes make them hard to relate to, and the book has a muddled message. The new book sold well at first (mostly based on the reputation of the author and the classic status of *Mockingbird* in film and literature), but it will not come close to the thirty million copies that Lee's first book sold. After its release, many bookstores offered refunds to disappointed fans. *Go Set a Watchman* will not be taught in many high school classrooms, except perhaps for the color it adds to the brilliance of the original.

This is the power of bringing in the perspective of a second person. It's the difference between a life- and world-changing classic and a disappointing flop.

Anyone who has ever worked with an editor on any type of project knows who is in charge—the final decisions still remain, however uncomfortably, with the creator—but in order to create something truly great, you must submit yourself and your work to this feedback process. Whether it's with an investor, an executive with green-lighting power, or an editor, at some point the work must leave your hands.

I mentioned the multiplatinum recording artist Adele earlier. After she finished preparing and writing the demos for the follow-up album to her record-breaking *21*, she reached out to her producer, Rick Rubin, to let him know she thought she was ready to begin the final step of recording. He listened to her quietly and had just one reply: "I don't believe you." As Adele later told *Rolling Stone*, "When he said it, I couldn't work out if I was, like, devastated, going to cry my eyes out. And then I just said, 'I don't really believe myself right now, so I'm not surprised you fucking said that.'"

Adele went back to the drawing board—for two *years* of additional work. The tribute to that work is paid in two places. First, the title is *25* instead of *27*, even though Adele had planned to name the album after her age when it was released. More compelling, the fans paid the ultimate compliment: 3.4 million copies sold in the first week alone, smashing the previous record by nearly a million units (set by NSYNC in 2000, in what was supposed to be the high-water mark of the physical record business).

What are the chances that your prototype is perfect the first time? *The Great Gatsby* was rejected several times. WD-40 is named after the forty attempts it took its creators to nail the working formula. None of my books were immediately accepted by my publisher—and they were right to kick them back at me. In being forced to go back to the manuscript, I got the books to where they needed to be. I know that now, but at the time it was infuriating to be told, "It's not quite there yet."*

As infuriating as it may be, we must be rational and fair about our own work. This is difficult considering our conflict of interest—which is to say, the ultimate conflict of interest: We made it. The way to balance that conflict of interest is to bring in people who are objective. Ask yourself: What are the chances that I'm right and everyone else in the world is wrong? We'll be better off at least *considering* why other people have concerns, because the reality is, truth is almost always somewhere in the middle.

When it comes to feedback, I think Neil Gaiman's advice captures the right attitude: "Remember: When people tell you something's wrong or doesn't work for them, they are almost always right. When they tell you exactly what they think is wrong and how to fix it, they are almost always wrong."

Only you know how to fix it—but you'll only find out what's wrong if you open yourself up to collaboration and input. I love Y Combinator's logic around its preference for startups with more than one founder. The reason? If you can't successfully work with

---

* I am adding in this footnote to mark what is my fifth submission of the manuscript for this book. How many passes and rounds of editing that constitutes is impossible to track, but it means I've heard the "not there yet" response at least four times. Will I make it this time? I don't know, but I'll keep trying until I do.

someone else (and no one wants to partner with you), that already says something about the project and your style. And even in a single CEO situation, doesn't the executive run the big decisions by a board of trusted advisers or directors?

Too many people are uninterested in submitting to such an arrangement or asking these tough questions. I saw it recently with a client of my firm. They hired us for several months of marketing, having sold us on a product that was supposedly ready for launch. As I dug into the product, however, I discovered a number of fundamental problems. It was similar to other existing apps, it was difficult to explain, and it seemed to address only a somewhat esoteric inconvenience for a nonexistent user base—or perhaps more accurately a user base of one: its creator. The founder was just so personally excited about it, he oversold what was actually there.

As my team and I worked to explain this to him, presenting a number of solutions to the obvious issues and advising that he seriously consider holding off on the launch, I received an abrupt email: He no longer wished to work together and was forfeiting the rather large retainer he'd paid.

It was his baby (and his money), so he was free to do what he wished, and I always try to consider where I might have gone wrong in an interaction. Was I too blunt? Was I just trying to buy myself time? Was I projecting? In this case, I wasn't—and I wasn't wrong either. With no real market, the service drifted and failed to get traction. It ultimately shut down, taking several million dollars' worth of funding with it. The company would have been far better off if it had solicited this kind of feedback or done this kind of thinking early on in the project. The problem was that they believed they were ready to start marketing, and therefore were unwilling to consider feedback that felt like it was taking them backward.

I recall this scenario each time I get painful or untimely feedback on my own projects. Do I feel like overriding this feedback because it's wrong, I ask myself, or is it because I don't want to hit pause and do more work? It's also a cautionary warning to me against telling myself I am "done" too early. I want to prolong that introspective review phase. Because it may just save me from finding out my project was dead on arrival come launch day.

Conversely, I look to the mercurial but incredibly successful author and entrepreneur James Altucher as a positive example of how to respond to feedback. When we worked on his book *Choose Yourself*, he came to us with what he thought was a complete manuscript and an aggressive release schedule. He was self-publishing, so all the advice was optional—he was free to do as he liked. But when we came back with clear feedback that he was not ready to launch, he listened. We subjected him to some sixteen rounds of edits over a six-month period, including a complete restructuring, the removal of four chapters entirely, and the addition of two new chapters at his editor's request. He never complained—even when it probably hurt. The result was a seminal self-improvement book that *USA Today* has called one of the twelve best business books of all time, with 600,000 copies sold, and it still moves 50,000 copies per year.

Every project needs to go through this process. Whether it's with an editor or a producer or a partner or a group of beta users or just through your own relentless perfectionism—whatever form it takes is up to you. But getting outside voices is crucial. The fact is, most people are so terrified of what an outside voice might say that they forgo opportunities to improve what they are making. Remember: Getting feedback requires humility. It demands that you subordinate your thoughts about your project and your love for it and entertain the idea that someone else might have a valuable thing or two to add.

Nobody creates flawless first drafts. And nobody creates better second drafts without the intervention of someone else. Nobody.

Polish and Perfect, Test and Retest

Not only should you be testing your project as you create it, you must most seriously test your creation as it begins to resemble a final product. So you know what you have—so you can improve it. So you know what you have—so that you might figure out what to do with it. So you know what you have—so you can adjust your expectations.

The songwriter Max Martin, who has written for everyone from Céline Dion to Taylor Swift to Bon Jovi and Adele, subjects his nearly finished songs to something he calls the LA Car Test, where he blares the song through the stereo of a car racing up and down a beautiful stretch of the Pacific Coast Highway in Los Angeles. *How does it sound? What does it add to the experience?* These are the questions he asks himself during the scenic drive. Why? Because he understands that that's what his music is *for*: to brighten people's days, to invigorate their drives, and to heighten their ordinary life experiences.*

Music, after all, is meant for the world, not the recording studio. In Rich Cohen's amazing biography of the Rolling Stones, he tells a story about Mick Jagger arguing with an engineer about which song would work best as a single. You need to hear it on the radio to know, the engineer said. But he lamented that by the time

---

* If you think Max Martin's music is too contemporary, well, I've heard that Metallica's James Hetfield and Lars Ulrich claim to have used "car test" for at least two decades. If you've ever heard their song "Fuel" while driving, you can see how it works.

you do, it is too late. The legend has it that the Stones' manager overheard this conversation and called up a local DJ and had him play the song early. Even if we don't have that kind of pull—and even if that never happened—we can still appreciate the brilliant understanding of the music business. It's not about what *you* like best; it's about what will sound best to the fans.

Max Martin's test is a way around that, and it addresses the same problem. Listening to the radio in the car on one of the most beautiful drives in the world, he is putting himself in the position of his ideal audience. He is asking: Does this create a valuable experience for them?

If a song doesn't pass Martin's test, what do you think he does with it? Proceed anyway and hope that the results were wrong? Of course not. He keeps working on it until it is fixed. Even if he wants to be done, even if the deadlines are bearing down on him.

We have to have this kind of discipline. The discipline required to hit pause and return to our prospective studios until the work meets the standards we've set for ourselves and that the fans have for us. We need to have our own test: Does a summary of the book work as a talk? Are the early users you've given prototypes to already addicted to their early versions of the product? Does what you made scratch your own itch in a way that suggests it will do the same for others?

The test for every product will be different, and so will the polish and tweaks we apply in response to the feedback. Yet nothing can replace taking the time to do this. We could come up with the most amazing song title or package it in the most beautiful album cover, but if the work doesn't do the job, what good will any of it be? That's why we work with our editors. That's why we test and retest, polish and perfect. Even when we'd like to be done, even when we're ready to move on, we don't stop until we've passed the test.

One Sentence, One Paragraph, One Page

There is a fundamental question of knowledge that goes all the way back to Plato and Socrates: If you don't know what you're looking for, how will you know if you've found it?

For creative projects, we wrestle with something similar at this stage in the process. Yes, we're editing and improving and refining and testing to see the results of these efforts, but we're not just doing these things for their own sake. We're certainly not doing it for the fun of it. We're working to get somewhere.

But where?

That's not a rhetorical question—there is a real answer, one that is unique to every project.

Sometime after the bulk of the creative production is done but before a work is fully wrapped up, a creator must step back and ask: "OK, what was I trying to make here? Did I get there? What do I need to change or fix in order to successfully do so?"

Again, I don't think *just* thinking about that question is the way to do it. Amazon has developed an internal culture that encourages physically writing out ideas, policies, suggestions, problems, and solutions—*write to think* is their belief. For that reason, Amazon actually requires managers who are launching a new product to write a press release about it *before* the idea is even given the green light. If they can't come up with a way to express their idea in exciting and compelling terms at this early stage, well, thank God it was caught in time before they launched *that dud*.

A similar exercise that I like to do with all my projects is one I call "One Sentence, One Paragraph, One Page." It goes like this:

Put the website or the beta version of your app or your manuscript aside and grab a piece of paper or open a blank Word document. Then, with fresh eyes, attempt to write out exactly what your project is supposed to be and to do in . . .

One sentence.

One paragraph.

One page.

This is a ———— that does ————. This helps people ————.

Fill in this template at the three varying lengths. It's best to do this exercise in the third person, creating a bit of artificial distance from the project so you can't fall back on, "Well, I think that . . ." Deal with facts instead.

If I may go off on a tangent for a minute, perhaps the most essential part of the sentence above with blanks is the first one— the part that says *what* the project is. Is it a book? Is it a big-budget Hollywood movie? Is it an experimental piece of modern art? In short, *What genre does it fit in?*

Genre matters. If you've written a great rock album but more than one of the songs on it are about Jesus, people are going to put it in the Christian rock genre. If that's your intention, fantastic. If it isn't, you might want to make some changes. If you're attempting to write a definitive Pulitzer Prize–worthy biography of a famous historical figure but it's only 126 pages, you've probably violated the unspoken qualifications of that genre of work. Is this a coffee shop or a coworking space or a members-only private club? It probably can't be all three—not without confusing or alienating the customers who are looking for just one of those options.

When your proposition to prospective customers is, "This is like [random genre] mixed with [random genre] with a little bit of [third random genre]," do you know what they hear? They hear confusion. Lightly fictionalizing your real insider experiences working on Wall Street into a novel doesn't give you *twice* the audience—say, fiction lovers and business types. It may actually give you half, because you've openly violated the basic conventions of two well-defined spaces. Now, it's unlikely you'll get media coverage for your very real portrayals of what goes on inside the hedge fund world, *and* you'll have trouble getting your average fiction reader to get excited about your fairly mundane plot or to understand exactly why any of what you've written about matters.

That's not to say you can't or shouldn't break rules with your work—remember, being bold and brave is important. But you need to know that this will likely make your job harder—and you'll need to compensate for it in various ways during the creative process, in your packaging and positioning, and certainly in your marketing. In a podcast discussion with screenwriter Brian Koppelman, Seth Godin explained, "Everything that has a clear path to commercial success is in a genre." We need to be able to put things into categories so we know where they fit. And you as the creator need to be clear and honest with yourself about where this work is going to fit for people.

That's why we do this exercise. So we know where we fit. We know what expectations we're setting and what we're going to have to do to meet them (which in some cases may require us to be twice as good just to make up for how unclear our proposition is).

(And that ends my genre tangent.)

When you know what genre you're in and you know what you're trying to accomplish, it becomes clearer which decisions matter and which don't. Jon Favreau once explained in an interview that as he was beginning to put together the pieces for the movie *Iron Man* he decided that his vision depended entirely on Robert Downey Jr. receiving the starring role. The rest of the decisions—the other actors, how to shoot the movie, the gear they'd need—would be clear if that happened. You could say his one sentence was: "Robert Downey Jr. is Iron Man." (Or perhaps in longer form: "We're doing a big-budget superhero movie, but it all hinges on Robert Downey Jr. being an unconventional but badass Iron Man.")

Favreau's singular insistence helped create one of the most valuable franchises in the history of film, but you can imagine how, without it, he might have been tempted to consider the notes and suggestions of the studio executives who wanted something different. This is why creators must know which variable(s) the project will hinge on. They must know which conventions of the genre they are observing and which ones they are taking a risk on by tweaking or subverting. They must understand—even if it is some vague gut notion—what they are making and what they are aiming for. If they do, the rest can be lined up against it. If they don't, how will they ever know if they've done it? How else will everything that comes after—from the movie poster to the marketing—come together?

It may take several drafts to get this exercise right; it might also necessitate going back and refining the product itself. In forcing ourselves through this process, we also force ourselves to explain succinctly what we have, what it does, and why anyone should care. If we're not able to, then it says something about the potential viability of this thing we are creating and our ability to explain it to the audience.

The most important part of the process is comparing the results of the exercise against the product we've made. Does your one-pager really describe what makes your screenplay worth producing? Would your one sentence capture an investor's attention in an elevator? You might find that, yes, your answers are compelling, but the work itself does not rise to meet the proposition they promote. Alternatively, you might find that the work is a lot more complex and important than your encapsulation suggests. If that's the case—if your product is great but your one-pager is blah—you probably need to rethink how you're talking about it. Perhaps you don't truly understand the topic well enough yet.

This is where an editor (or any early eyes on the project) comes into play again. You say to them: "Here's what I've been aiming for. Do you think I am close? What do I need to change with my [writing, design, music, art, etc.] to get where I'm trying to go?"

Too rarely, creators forget to consciously stop and compare their first attempt against their goal. Often they can't even articulate where they were trying to end up and what that would really look like if they did.

Instead, they wing it. The result? A name and tagline way out of alignment with where the project ended up. Or a passionate, long-winded description of the work . . . utterly indecipherable to anyone other than the creator. Or, worse, a product pitch that bores you out of your mind because they haven't put the time or thought into making it exciting.

Who Are You Aiming For?

In the raw, conceptual phase, it was essential that you had some idea who you were making your work for—an unaimed arrow rarely hits a target. Now, just as you did with your one sentence, it's time to return to the intended audience—to see whether you've actually produced something they need. Then, depending on that answer, adjust either the audience or the product until there's a perfect match.

The intended audience is the final blank in the "This is a _____ that does _____" exercise. It's what ties the rest all together: "This is a _____ that does _____ *for* _____."

I've asked a lot of people that question over the years, and the list of wrong answers would fill volumes. A few particularly egregious ones are common:

- "Everyone"
- "You know, smart people"
- "The kind of people who read Malcolm Gladwell"
- "Myself"

The problem with those answers is not just that they are vague ("smart people") or ridiculous ("myself"); it's that such audiences *don't exist.* There is no convention where Malcolm Gladwell fans get together.* They don't all read the same website. Just as every politician has to create his or her own coalition in order to win, no creator can magically inherit the audience of another. Whatever you're making is not for "everyone" either—not even the Bible is for everyone. For yourself? I know you're not going to be satisfied selling just *one* copy.

At least those answers are plainly wrong. The most common response is even more alarming. It's the creator who answers the audience question with:

"I don't know. I haven't thought much about it."

If you haven't thought about who you are trying to reach, then what *have* you thought about? Presumably you have some vision of people purchasing or using this thing you've spent all your time making. How could you not know who they are? It's not going to happen by accident!

---

* It is interesting to think of all the academics who complain about Malcolm Gladwell "popularizing" their work. What they're really saying is: "He knows how to reach people better than we do. He is better at articulating our findings to the world than we are."

Contrary to what most people think about the viral content BuzzFeed is famous for, its founder Jonah Peretti has said that every article BuzzFeed publishes isn't supposed to be read by millions of people. Yes, every post is supposed to spread socially, but it is supposed to be viral *for its intended audience*, whatever the size. Doing that requires knowing who that is *while* the content is being made.

When Susan Cain published her book about introversion, she had a very specific audience in mind: introverts. This was also a traditionally underserved audience, which is even better from a positioning perspective (when supply is down, demand is high). The result was *Quiet: The Power of Introverts in a World That Can't Stop Talking*, a publishing sensation that has not only moved more than two million copies, but also spurred courses, leadership consulting, and a viral TED Talk that has been watched more than fourteen million times. But imagine if she'd poorly branded or defined that initial product. Imagine if, in an early manuscript, she had not clearly defined what introversion was or provided enough practical tips and strategies—and her editor had allowed her to get away with it. Do you think she would have had the same kind of success?

In the same way, the *Left Behind* series is obviously for Christians. Its films, novels, graphic novels, video games, and albums are preaching with a very specific choir in mind.

Cannibal Holocaust is a dark and twisted horror film meant for the most extreme horror fans—it's certainly not for highbrow critics or average theatergoers.

The Blue Collar Comedy tour (with well-known Southern comedians), the Three Amigos tour (with well-known Latino comedians), the Original Kings of Comedy tour (with well-known African-American comedians), and the Axis of Evil Comedy tour (with well-known Middle Eastern comedians) were all aimed at very specific ethnic and social groups.

Since 2009, ABC has taken a similar approach with its weeknight programming. The network developed a series of family sitcoms that target discrete segments of their overall viewership. *Modern Family* (since 2009) is about a mixed family featuring different types of modern relationships. *The Middle* (since 2009) is about a struggling Midwestern working-class family. *The Goldbergs* (since 2013) is a nostalgic show about family life in the 1980s. *Blackish* (since 2014) is about a suburban, upper-middle-class black family. *Fresh Off the Boat* (since 2015) is about an immigrant Asian family trying to make it in suburban Florida.

Did those projects have additional audiences? Absolutely—indeed, the creators hoped for crossover appeal—but their strength was rooted in the narrow, mostly underserved demographics they were specifically designed for.

For my first book, *Trust Me, I'm Lying*, I knew I was specifically targeting media folks, publicists, and a new generation of social media employees. Here's the exact language I laid out in that proposal:

> Jobs in social media are one of the hottest-growing sectors in the economy. . . . This growing workforce eagerly eats up whatever information it can learn from—these young workers have not yet begun to grasp how the industry really works because the industry is only in its infancy. Fundamentally different from the preachy-and-useless books from media critics and "—for Dummies" style how-to books, **Confessions of a Media Hit Man** is not only an instructional manual for mastering the wild world of social media but an honest warning of the dangers—written by someone who

has personally been there. Marketed as intended, **Confessions of a Media Hit Man** is poised to inspire and define a generation of workers in the style of its predecessor, David Ogilvy's *Confessions of an Advertising Man*, which became the bible of the advertising and public relations industry, is still in print more than fifty years after publication, and sold more than one million copies.

The title of the book eventually changed, and the book was written and rewritten over the course of a year in order to fulfill my admittedly grandiose pitch, but the audience stayed the same. I had to work my ass off to hit that target—and that was possible only because I had first articulated said target.

You must be able to explicitly say who you are building your thing for. You must know what you are aiming for—you'll miss otherwise. You need to know this so you can make the decisions that go into properly positioning the project for them. You need to know this so you can edit and refine the work until it's so utterly awesome that your target group cannot resist buying it. Marketing then becomes a matter of finding where those people are and figuring out the best way to reach them.

Is Bigger Better?

As creators, we seem to fall into two camps: Either we have dreams of utter dominance and stardom, or we retain a sort of hipster disdain for popularity. I think both of these extremes are silly.

I think of popularity as a set of concentric circles (though it does happen that a product might mean wildly different things to different groups). Each small audience is contained inside a potentially larger audience. Young male New Yorkers who love heavy metal are a subset of guys who listen to rock music, for example, just as the audience of expecting mothers contains within it expecting mothers who work from home.

I was once at a talk where the founder of Justin's Peanut Butter was asked why he started with creamy peanut butter instead of crunchy. His answer was impressive: In tests he'd run, Justin found that folks who liked crunchy peanut butter were more than happy to eat creamy, yet folks who liked creamy peanut butter would rather have *nothing* than eat crunchy. Starting with creamy allowed him to reach both audiences—and potentially expand into the other market later—but if he'd started with crunchy, he'd have had no chance. For creators, it's typically easier to reach the smaller, better-defined group. If you reach the smaller group and wow them, there will be many opportunities to spread outward and upward. (In many cases, your fans will do this for you, recommending your work to people like them, but not exactly like them.) The key to this is to service the *core audience* first and do so in a way that does not alienate the others—only then can you emanate outwardly from the center.

Lady Gaga crafted her sound, her persona, and her fan base at gay bars, clubs, and burlesque shows in New York and San Francisco. From there she was able to bring that theatrical performance and sound to dance clubs, the fashion crowd, and then eventually to the mainstream. There's actually a famous line from an episode of *Sex and the City*, written long before Lady Gaga's career was even conceived, that charts her exact trajectory: "First come the gays. Then the girls. Then . . . the industry."

Many massively popular artists have followed this path in their own way.

Regardless, you must start somewhere—ideally somewhere quantifiable. By which I mean: Who is buying the first one thousand copies of this thing? Who is coming in on the first day? Who is going to claim our first block of available dates? Who is buying our first production run?

The number is going to differ for every kind of product and for each different niche. But there are rules of thumb. For books, the superagent and publishing entrepreneur Shawn Coyne (Robert McKee, Jon Krakauer, Michael Connelly) likes to use ten thousand readers as his benchmark. That's what it takes, in his experience, for a book to successfully break through and for the ideas in it to take hold. Remember, *a lot* is not a number. The famous music promoter and later movie producer Jerry Weintraub (*The Karate Kid* and the *Ocean's* series) has a good story about this in his memoir *When I Stop Talking, You'll Know I'm Dead*. He'd had the idea to rent out Yankee Stadium for a celebrity softball game with Elvis. On a day the stadium wasn't in use, the owner of the Yankees took Weintraub out onto the field and forced him to look at all the empty seats—each one symbolizing someone who would have to be marketed to, sold, and serviced for his event to work. It was a formative lesson, he said. "Whenever I am considering an idea, I picture the seats rising from second base at Yankee Stadium. Can I sell that many tickets? Half that many? Twice that many?"

With a concrete number in mind, it's a lot easier to establish and empathize with what your audience is going to need. And, more to the point, to anticipate what they might want to see in order to be attracted to what you're doing.

A formative lesson for me in this regard came when I was a research assistant to Robert Greene. He would send me off to find stories he could use in his writing, and I would come back with options I thought might work. At one point, looking at all the material I had spent weeks gathering, he said something to the effect of: "Ryan, all your stories are from nineteenth-century white guys. That's not going to work." He wanted a diversity of examples in his work *so that every reader would feel included.* I remember just how incredibly selective Robert was when choosing the various masters he would profile in his book *Mastery.* They had to have different jobs—a fighter pilot, a boxing coach, a robotics inventor, a prize-winning artist—and have diverse backgrounds, genders, and cultures. What I came to realize about his brilliant approach was that he wanted every single reader to find someone they could relate to in his books. He wanted them to see themselves across his pages. (There is nothing more badass for a reader than to see themselves as the hero.) He also wanted them to be able to see their friends, family, and colleagues—so they could recommend it to them.

You must create room for the audience to inhabit and relate to the work. You must avoid the trap of making this about you—because, remember, you won't be the one buying it. In that way, Robert's insistence on diversity wasn't coming only from his very real sense of fairness and tolerance. There was a genius business logic to his choices as well: Each master was a conduit into a new community to whom the book might appeal and be promoted. This was a marketing asset—or rather, a pre-marketing asset—built directly in during the writing and editing phases.

Are you really sure that you have features and scenes and material that are relevant to your core audience? And to your potential audiences? And to your audience's potential audiences? If you don't have this, then you need to fix it now, or may God help you. Because you're going to need divine intervention.

Positioning, Packaging, and the Pitch

Not too long ago, we used to care about *who* was making something—what studio was releasing a project, what publisher was behind a book, what label was behind an album. It meant something to be signed by Death Row Records or to star in an MGM picture. This reputational weight reduced some of the burdens of marketing. But as production costs plummeted over time, the number of people who could form a charity, write a book, produce a short film, or start a company skyrocketed. The democratization of production was great news—it empowered people like you and me. The bad news is that it empowered millions of other people too.

Today, in order to even have a chance at people's attention, your project has to seem as good as or better than all the others. Three critical variables determine whether that will happen: the Positioning, the Packaging and the Pitch.

Positioning is what your project is and who it is for.

Packaging is what it looks like and what it's called.

The Pitch is the sell—how the project is described and what it offers to the audience.

Each is essential. Each feeds into the others. Done properly, your work will scream: "Pick me—forsake the others. This is urgent!" Done haphazardly, your work simply says: "Bleh." Or, worse, it says: "Don't bother. My creator didn't care enough to explain why you should care. This thing is like all the others."

The last impression any work can afford to make is: "Oh, that is just some random thing a random person made." Work that is going to sell and sell must appear as good as, or better than, the *best* stuff out there. Because that's who you're competing with: not the other stuff being released right now, but everything that came before you. A new TV show is competing with on-demand episodes of *Breaking Bad* and *Seinfeld* and *The Wire*. A new book is competing with Sophocles and John Grisham. Your game is competing not just against Angry Birds or Words with Friends but against all the other demands that exist on people's time. And remember that the creators and owners of those projects have worked incredibly hard so that everything about their work—from the box it's in to the poster on the wall to the logo or the name—is perfect.

Bret Taylor, one of the engineers responsible for creating Google Maps, explains that breaking through is not as simple as just making something great. "You might be ten times better," he says, "but your customers may not even understand why it's important that you're better." How could they be expected to understand if they haven't tried it yet? That's why it's critical that you be able not only to clearly and concisely explain who and what you are, but also to *show* it, too.

Infinite shelf space means there is no availability bias. It means that audiences are busy and entitled and making split-second decisions about whether to consume this or *that*. How you present yourself has an enormous influence over whether you will be chosen or ignored. It's how you teach people that you are better. It's how you separate yourself from the others. It's the face and the name tag you put on your work.

The differences between doing it well and doing it poorly are enormous. The same article with a slightly different headline can have a tenfold spread in readership. One stands out; the other doesn't. That saying "You can't judge a book by its cover"? It's total nonsense. Of course you can judge a book by its cover—*that's why books have covers*. They're designed to catch people's attention and draw them toward the work—and away from all the other works that stand equal on the shelf.

When it comes to attracting an audience, the creators who take the time to get their positioning and packaging right—who don't just go with their first instinct and *hope*—are the ones who will win.

This may cost you some money and time, but it's worth it in the long run. When Steve Jobs launched NeXT—his first company after Apple fired him—he spent something like $100,000 on a logo from one of the best designers in the world. When Marissa Mayer was in charge of product at Google, she once tested forty-one different shades of blue to see which one users responded to best—because at a large scale, those differences matter. One of my clients, Tim Ferriss, spends hundreds of hours rigorously testing everything from his title to his cover ideas to his *chapter* titles. This process produced the title for his first book—the runaway mega-bestseller *The 4-Hour Workweek*—and set him up with perfect branding for an entire franchise (*The 4-Hour Body*, *The 4-Hour Chef*). You get a sense of what generates a response and what doesn't by creating multiple cover options and bringing in a sample of friends with good taste and expertise to vote on them (tools like SurveyMonkey and Google Docs make this quite easy). Another client, Neil Strauss, spent nearly a year agonizing over whether to title one of his books *Game Over* or *The Truth*—both titles had advantages and disadvantages, and he knew it would take time and brainpower to figure out which was best. I remember shouting in exasperation at one point, "Neil, *just choose!*" But he's the multimillion-bestselling author for a reason.

Most of the time, however, the opposite is true. I see creators who have had their design work done on Fiverr.com (for five dollars) or had a friend (or some person they knew) make their website for a few dollars. I *cringe* when I see these projects. It's clear the creators have taken a shortcut or settled. "Why'd you choose that name?" "My daughter liked it." "How do you like your cover?" "It's good enough." "The design of this feature is confusing." "I know, but we'll fix it later." Obviously, these are choices anyone is free to make, but they are more in line with a side project than a career-defining would-be perennial seller. It's certainly not how professionals would treat their work.

Looks are important, but they are only a fraction of this discussion. At some point in every project I work on, I find myself recommending that the creator take the time to consult the book *The 22 Immutable Laws of Marketing.* The first seven laws of this classic marketing tome deal with the art of positioning and packaging. Not branding or style, but something deeper and also broader.

Law 2, for instance, is about the art of categorization. "If you can't be first in a category," the law states, "set up a new category you can be first in."

Charity:water is an organization that excels in this regard. I'm not simply talking about its unusual name—which is unique and attention-grabbing—but rather its unusual structure, which helps it stand out and attract donations. Following Law 2 to the letter, Charity:water invented its own category of charity—in which every dollar you donate goes directly to people in need. You see, Charity:water split itself into two "separate" organizations: one that builds wells in developing countries and another that handles the administrative costs for the charity. This clever positioning trick allows the organization to claim that 100 percent of your donations goes to building wells (thus differentiating its structure from most other charities). Ultimately, the organization costs the same amount to run; the only difference is an artificial separation of bank accounts. But building this distinction into the messaging from day one made Charity:water stand out from so many other organizations. It's the only one where *all* the money you donate helps people in need!

My point is that positioning isn't simply a matter of moving words around on the page. It can be taking action or making a structural change in your product or organization. It's also *doing* the things that allow you to have the market fit you need to stand out and be interesting.

Yet, creators will often spend years making something but then rush through their descriptive copy in an hour, or they'll rubber-stamp some "options" sent over by the design team. They might have spent months producing a film with hundreds of collaborators, but they'll approve the film's artwork in an afternoon by themselves. This is a strange statement of priorities given that a huge portion of the film's potential audience will see the poster long before the movie. The same goes for the Amazon page of a book or the box your $500 product sits in on store shelves.

A great package on a great product is what creates an explosive reaction. For instance, J. D. Salinger's *Catcher in the Rye* sold decently when it was first published in hardcover, but then sold over 1.25 *million* copies in its early pulp paperback edition. The provocative cover, designed by James Avati ("the Rembrandt of Pulp"), had a lot to do with it. In his version, Holden Caulfield is standing outside a strip club and the blurb reads, "This unusual book may shock you, will make you laugh, and may break your heart—but you will never forget it!" It's ironic that the book's literary reputation today is partly a result of its massive down-market popularity at the time. It's also funny that Salinger *hated* the cover and eventually redesigned it himself. (That's the literary luxury of an author who has sold millions of copies.)

Meanwhile, the wrong packaging can drag a wonderful project down or prevent it from reaching fans who might otherwise like it. Imagine if your product were for one group—say, successful adults with disposable income—but your branding violated what they expected in terms of style and appearance? This was exactly why the startup Wealthfront, now with more than one billion dollars under management, changed its name from KaChing (!!!). *Pretty Woman* was original titled *3,000* but was renamed, in part, to match Roy Orbison's song in the soundtrack. The Tom Cruise cult hit *Edge of Tomorrow* was rebranded to *Live. Die. Repeat* when the studio discovered that the latter title, you know, actually explained what was awesome about the movie while the original title made it sound like just another action flick.

It's not easy to change your name or hire a new design firm midway through a project. But it's far better to feel the pain now instead of later, when despite all your efforts the marketing just *isn't working*.

Consider how someone would describe your book, movie, restaurant, campaign, candidacy—whatever—at a party. Consider someone trying to tell someone else about it in just 140 characters. What would they say? Will they feel stupid saying it? It's a _____ that does _____ for _____. Have you made filling in those blanks as easy and exciting as possible? Have you done the hard work for them?

All of that leads to the most essential part of packaging and positioning: *the pitch*. That is: What's your sell for this thing? How do you tell people what it is and why they should care?

There is an infamous letter written by Harvey Weinstein, the movie producer behind projects like *Pulp Fiction* and *Gangs of*

New York, to Errol Morris, the brilliant documentary filmmaker responsible for movies like the Oscar-winning *The Fog of War*. With one of his early films, *The Thin Blue Line*, Morris was apparently doing a poor job explaining the movie in interviews. Weinstein was not pleased, and wrote to Morris with this admonition:

> Speak in short one-sentence answers and don't go in with all the legalese. Talk about the movie as a movie and the effect it will have on the audience from an emotional point of view. If you continue to be boring, I will hire an actor in New York to pretend that he's Errol Morris. . . . Keep it short and keep selling it because that's what is going to work for you, your career and the film.

In other words, Errol Morris might have made an awesome documentary, but it wasn't going to succeed unless he could figure out how to communicate what was awesome about it to others. He had to explain to the media and to critics and to every other kind of gatekeeper why they should care—so that the public could be in a position to hear about it in the first place (and then care themselves). Weinstein helped him fix that with this suggested exchange:

> Q: What is this movie about?
>
> A: It's a mystery that traces an injustice. It's scarier than NIGHTMARE ON ELM STREET. It's like a trip to the Twilight Zone. People have compared it to IN COLD BLOOD with humor.

The reason I wanted to walk you through the One Sentence, One Paragraph, One Page exercise was not only for your own internal clarity. At some point in the near future (the third section of this book), you're going to have to describe to other human beings *what this project is* in an exciting and compelling way. You're going to need to explain to reporters, prospective buyers or investors, publishers, and your own fans:

Who this is for

Who this is not for

Why it is special

What it will do for them

Why anyone should care

The one sentence and one paragraph can be taken and tweaked for public consumption. It's creating a literal elevator pitch: You've got fifteen seconds to catch an important person's attention. When you were creating or when this was all in your head, you could get away with a sloppy approximation: "It's a book about _____." "I'm writing a movie about ____." Well, in an elevator, when you're actually pitching people, you're also going to need to explain what _____ is, why there is a market for it, and why people should read it. My "book about Stoic philosophy," for example, had to become "a book that uses the ancient formula of the Emperor Marcus Aurelius to teach people how to not only overcome obstacles but *thrive because of them*." The diner you're trying to raise money to open needs to become "a new spin on an American institution and the perfect restaurant for this cool neighborhood, which for too long has lacked a place for people to have a casual meal—whether a sandwich for lunch, a late dinner, or a hangover-ending breakfast with friends."

None of these choices can be rushed. There is no room for compromise or "good enough" here. You might be inclined to just go with your first instinct and be done with it. Your investors, your publishers, your employees, your family and friends might push you to finish quickly and get it out into the world. They don't understand that you may have only one shot at this. The choices you make here can't be compensated for in the marketing later. In fact, *they are the marketing.*

In this way, you must be willing to be a big enough jerk—ahem, enough of a perfectionist—to say: "No, we're not moving on from here until we get this right." Because you know that nothing else will matter—the quality of your product, the strength of your marketing—if the premise and the pitch of the product are wrong.

Why Are You Doing This?

What is it that you want? What is truly motivating you? What are you trying to accomplish with this project? The answer should be clear by now: I am making a _____ that does _____ for _____ because _____.

The "why" doesn't need to be public—but if you can't define your goal for yourself, how will you know if you've achieved it? How will you know how to make decisions in situations where that goal is threatened or jeopardized? How will you know how to turn down the exciting distractions that might take you away from it? How will you know that all your effort was worth it and the effort was at least noble if—God forbid—the plan doesn't turn out exactly as expected?

As in: I'm writing a book about depression for the millions of Americans who suffer in silence every year because if I can save a single life, the entire project will be worth it. I am writing a summer anthem for teenagers that makes them roll down the windows and turn the radio up because I miss that feeling and want to bring people together. I am creating an app that helps women track and monitor their pregnancy because there wasn't anything like it during mine and I know I would have paid a ton of money for it. I am writing a film about the poker craze that captures what this world is really like because it's a huge scene that everyone else has ignored and I know they will love it.

Elon Musk knows that his mission is to get a human being on Mars, and he believes that the future of humanity rests on it. That's the kind of clarity you want.

Some of our reasons will be serious, some will be self-interested or seemingly trivial—"No one's ever done this before, and I'd like to try"—but clarity of purpose and clarity of *goals* is essential.

I'll give you my explicit mission for *Trust Me, I'm Lying.* I told myself: I am writing an exposé of the media system that will shock and appall people who follow the news or are trying to market something—because I'm the only one in the world who can do it. I also consciously told myself that I was writing this book at this time (instead of later) because it was the right book to launch my writing career. I knew I would write more than one book in my career, but this was closest to my immediate expertise and had the greatest chance of commercial success. The secrets I carried were a weight on my chest that I wanted to remove, *and* I believed that the timing and priority made this the right moment to do it.

There are many different missions. Whatever yours is, it must be defined and articulated.

Once that has occurred, there is one last thing you must do. You must deliberately forsake all other missions. If your goal is to make a masterpiece, a perennial seller for a specific audience, it follows that you can't also hope that it is a trendy, of-the-moment side hustle. If your motivation is a selfless desire to reach a mistreated group, you shouldn't also be telling yourself that a big payday is around the corner. If you've committed to doing something incredibly difficult that countless others have failed at before, you probably also shouldn't be juggling five other projects at the same time. You'll need to put 100 percent of your resources toward this one.

Nothing has sunk more creators and caused more unhappiness than this: our inherently human tendency to pursue a strategy aimed at accomplishing one goal while *simultaneously* expecting to achieve other goals entirely unrelated.

Seneca was a famous Roman philosopher and playwright whose works were so beloved that a line of graffiti from his play *Agamemnon* remains preserved in ash on a two-thousand-year-old wall in Pompeii. Fittingly, he has some philosophical advice for any creator struggling to do something "great and supreme and nearly divine." In one of his essays, a perennial masterpiece still being sold two millennia after he penned it, Seneca wrote that what's required is "confidence in yourself and the belief that you are on the right path, and not led astray by the many tracks which cross yours of people who are hopelessly lost, though some are wandering not far from the true path."

An opera singer shouldn't compare her record sales to a pop group and wonder why she hasn't been invited on MTV. A sports team in a rebuilding phase doesn't judge itself against the best record in the league. A person on a singular mission can't be distracted; he can't chase every colored balloon he comes across. If your goal is to create a perennial seller, you can't measure yourself against people who aren't aiming for the same thing—you can't be endlessly checking industry charts or lists, and you can't be distracted by the trends and fancies of other creators who are hopelessly lost.

When the CEO of Snapper lawn mowers famously said no to selling cheap versions of his products to Walmart a few years ago, it was because the company had a firm understanding of its own goals (and the connections those goals had with their brand and audience). It wasn't just turning down the millions of dollars in the short term that would have made this decision difficult; it was that everyone else in his industry did business with Walmart. *You're supposed to play ball with them.* But what if your entire company is based on the support of local, independent retailers and having a stellar reputation for quality? What influence are you going to side with—what everyone thinks you should do or what you know is your real mission? He knew what he was trying to do, and that allowed him to make a tough decision.

Likewise, if you've fallen into the sway of tracking your fellow creators on social media or you check the charts every week to see what other people are doing, you're going to sap yourself of the discipline required to do what *you are trying to do.* Only idealists or masochists would think they can appeal to everyone and are entitled to everything. Only crazy people would compare themselves to people on totally different tracks.

With a perennial seller as your goal, the track is clear: *lasting impact and relevance.*

This will help in a number of decisions, some minor and some major. Consider: If you're looking at two different deals, one of which is for a lot more money and the other of which is with someone who can't afford to pay as much up front but who genuinely understands what you're trying to accomplish, take a pass on the money. If you have a launch date looming and everyone around you is "all systems go" but you feel some serious doubt that you're not ready, please make the difficult choice to stop the presses and take the time to get it right, even if it means extra costs. If you're deciding between two names—one that feels trendy, cool, and safe and the other risky but fully expressive of what you know in your heart is the truth of your project—go with the latter. Knowing what your goal is—having that crystal clear—allows you to know when to follow conventional wisdom and when to say "Screw it."

There are too many famous Steve Jobs anecdotes to count, but several of them revolve around one theme: his unwillingness to leave well enough alone. His products had to be perfect; they had to do what they promised, and then some. And even though deadlines loomed and people would have to work around the clock, he would regularly demand more from his teams than they thought they could provide. The result? The most successful company in the history of the world and products that inspire devotion that is truly unusual for a personal computer or cell phone.

Another Jobs lesson: He didn't think about what other people would do. He didn't think about what he *should* do. He did what he felt was right for the company over the long term. He wanted the computers to be beautiful down to the circuit boards, even though no one would ever see that. Consider your mission—consider each decision with some distance, from Cyril Connolly's perspective a decade out from now. Wouldn't you rather have done the difficult thing than taken a shortcut?

Coming to Terms with Commercialism

At this stage, there might be a voice in your head wondering: Isn't this all a little gross? I'm a creative person because I love art. It's my audience's job to figure out what to make of it. Won't I compromise my work by thinking of all this capitalistic positioning crap?

This is a trade-off that *every* artist struggles with. Bruce Springsteen had this inner struggle too—to be big but to produce great work—and in wrestling with it he created *Born to Run*:

> My heroes, from Hank Williams to Frank Sinatra to Bob Dylan, were popular musicians. They had hits. There was value in trying to connect with a large audience. . . . [But] artists with the ability to engage a mass audience are always involved in an inner debate as to whether it's worth it, whether the rewards compensate for the single-mindedness, energy and exposure necessary to meet the demands of the crowd.

This is the debate we all have. It'd be easier to just make our work and say: "Let it be what it may." Yet this leaves too much to chance and too much on the table. Our expression, if it is to have impact, must reach other people. As Chuck Klosterman wrote, even the most pretentious and elitist artist would not be satisfied if *no one* saw what they were making—if he was, "he'd sit in a dark room and imagine he wrote it already." Nabokov, a writer's writer if there ever was one, said it best: "Literature is not only fun, it is also business." To survive in business, you must make other people (and yourself) money. You must serve customers. To believe otherwise is *bad* business.

Too many creators are distracted by critics, by prizes, by buzz or media attention or impressing their friends, and they forget this. They forget their audience, customers, fans. The fashion designer Marc Ecko has good advice: We can't prioritize the gatekeepers (the media) over the goalkeepers (the audience). To do so is foolishly shortsighted.

We got into the creativity business to reach people. Why would we artificially limit that? The only reason to turn up your nose at growing your audience or increasing your reach is fear. It's easy to act superior. It's easy to say, "I don't care about any of that." It's easy not to try, because then you have a ready-made excuse.

A friend of mine, Jeff Goins, makes the distinction between starving artists and *thriving* artists. One adopts all the tropes and clichés of the bohemians and supposed purity. The other is resilient, ambitious, open-minded, and audience-driven. Who do you want to be? Which will propel your work the furthest?

One of the things I love about rap music is that there is none of this. Rappers don't just make music and "hope" they'll be successful. They've got hustle. Artists know that image and branding are just as important as the music itself if they want to sell millions *and* be known by millions. In one of his songs, Kanye West asks the audience what they think he raps for, "To push a fucking RAV4?" He wants to do it big—he wants more than to just survive making his art. Good for him.

"Selling out" is the label that so many creatives are afraid of being branded with. That's absurd—as though there were some single standard of what artistic credibility and audience should be. You alone are the judge of that. Perhaps to you success is a RAV4, whereas to someone else it's a Bentley. I bought my wife a RAV4 with the income from my books. I like to drive it sometimes. It's actually pretty nice. You know what that says about my work? Absolutely nothing. It's *a car*.

Don't let that inner hipster critic hold you back either. You cannot expect to sell unless you've put the work in and made the sacrifices and decisions that allow success to happen. You have to be ready for what comes next: the real marathon that is *marketing*.

One Last Thing

Most people are aware that Winston Churchill was both a politician and a statesman; fewer are aware of his brilliance as a writer or his passion for painting. He published his first book at twenty-three and his second at twenty-four, two works that made him an international celebrity at a young age. In his sixties, Churchill would begin a multivolume set titled *A History of the English-Speaking Peoples*, which took *twenty* years to finish and publish (he fought a world war in the middle of it). He would later win the Nobel Prize in literature. Though Churchill was not as talented as a painter, he found it to be a great source of personal satisfaction and expression—and he traveled with his brushes and paints wherever he went.

This was a man who knew how hard it was to create something, what it took to produce great work and then put it out into the world. No better words about the creative process have been produced than when he described starting a project as an adventure. "To begin with," he said, your project "is a toy and an amusement. Then it becomes a mistress, then it becomes a master, then it becomes a tyrant. The last phase is that just as you are about to be reconciled to your servitude, you kill the monster and fling it to the public."

That's where you are now. You've done your creative work. You began your editing and reviewing, and perhaps that sent you straight back to the creative phase for significant reworking. Finally, as you fine-tuned and polished and adjusted for your audience, you began to prepare yourself for the inevitable day of your release. How would you describe this project? What's special about it? What's its pitch? Who is it for? All those questions were designed to anticipate the questions you would one day get from the media and from retailers and customers.

Well, now that day is nearly here. It's time to put the pen down, back away from the computer, stop tweaking and fiddling. It's time to fling this thing to the public.

In the next half of this book, we're going to talk about how to reach as much of the public as possible. Before we do that, however, it's worth noting: Our work will soon leave our hands. Meaning: It will be out there for other people to judge. Not everyone will like it. Some may even hate it.

We must steel ourselves in advance for these reactions. The artist's life is hard. The road to a perennial seller is long—and it may seem, at times, that you're heading in the wrong direction and that the sidewalks are lined with hostile faces. No matter.

What we spent the first half of the book making—the effort we expended there—was intrinsically valuable. It was honorable, noble work. Whether the world immediately appreciates it bears no reflection on that. Be proud of yourself.

But only for a second. Because now our next job begins.

Part III

MARKETING

From Courting to Coverage, Pushing to Promotion

❊❊❊

Customers will not come just because you build it. You have to make that happen and it's harder than it looks.

—Peter Thiel

You've reached the halfway point of the creative journey. You did more than just have an idea; you actually made that idea into something real. You *sacrificed* to make it real. You spent time figuring out the specialness and why people should care. For years you dreamed that this day would come, and now it is here. You've been accepted into an elite club—you have created work that is both intrinsically and compellingly packaged and positioned.

Now the bad news: There's still a lot of competition out there left to beat.

We are fighting not just against our contemporaries for recognition, but against centuries of great art for an audience. Each new work competes for customers with everything that came before it and everything that will come after. How many new songs are featured in Spotify's New Music Friday playlist each week? How many of them do you ever hear again? How many films are submitted to Sundance each year? How many are selected? And the few dozen that do win are hardly out of the woods—they still need to find a buyer willing to distribute them, who in turn needs to figure how to sell them to an audience amid all the studio pictures coming out at the same time. Literally hundreds of films have been recognized by that film festival since it started in 1978, and only a very small percentage have been seen by a significant portion of the general public. That's a lot of great art ignored by a lot of people who have only so much time.

This has always been true. In 1842, a character in one of Balzac's novels, a journalist, observed that "the great problem for artists to solve is how to place themselves where they can be seen." If they don't solve this problem, they die and their work dies along with them. Being lost among all the noise is even more likely today than it was in the French author's time.

You can't be gassed now. There is too much left to do.

As I defined it in my book on growth hacking, marketing is anything that *gets* or *keeps* customers. That's what we must do now that our work is finished: sell and promote it to the audience we think it deserves.

Every creator faces the problem of "Who will enjoy what I have made?" Marketing is the solution. It's not only how you ensure your work finds its audience when it launches, but also how it will continue to find and have one as time passes. Marketing is both an art and a science, and must be mastered by all creators who hope their work will find traction. Without it, how is anyone going to hear about what you've made? Why should they choose it over any of the amazing other work that's out there? Especially if the makers of those works are themselves hustling to spread the word?

This book began with a criticism of the notion that creatives need to spend more time marketing and selling than they do making. I'm not contradicting myself by making marketing a priority now. I'm saying that the order in which you arrange these tasks matters. Marketing is the next essential step in the creation of a perennial seller.

Herb Cohen, considered one of the world's greatest negotiators, famously said, "You're better off with a great salesman and a mediocre product than with a masterpiece and a moron to sell it." Gun to my head, I might choose the former over the latter too. Better still would be to avoid that false dilemma altogether.

To have work that lasts, you can't have a mediocre product *or* be a moron. You have to be brilliant at all of it.

Marketing Is Your Job

In an interview, the novelist Ian McEwan once complained lightheartedly about what it was like to go out and market a book after spending all that time creating it: "I feel like the wretched employee of my former self. My former self being the happily engaged novelist who now sends me, a kind of brush salesman or double glazing salesman, out on the road to hawk this book. He got all the fun writing it. I'm the poor bastard who has to go sell it."

Considering how few people get to produce art for a living, and how much drudgery and "hawking" is involved in almost every other industry and profession, this seems like a rather privileged complaint. Who is going to sell your movie, your app, your artwork, your service if *not* you? Even if you pay someone else a lot of money, how hard are they really going to work?

Look around, Peter Thiel tells startup founders in his classic book *Zero to One*. "If you don't see any salespeople, *you're the salesperson*" (emphasis mine) for your product. Even if there are salespeople working for you, you're still the boss and will have to lead from the front.

Who should make the time if not you? What does it say that you're not willing to roll up your sleeves to get to work here? Name one person who should be more invested in the potential success of this project than you. (If you can name someone, bring him or her on as a partner right now!)

The idea that the world is waiting with bated breath for another movie, another book, another app? In fact, the whole idea behind perennial sellers is that the math overwhelmingly shows that people love classics from the recent and distant past. When Harper-Collins has an imprint called Harper Perennial, for instance, or when catalog albums are outselling new releases, it should tell you something: People are pretty happy with the old stuff.

To get them to like *your* stuff is no easy task, then. The idea that you won't have to work to sell your product is more than entitled.

" 'If you build it they will come' *can* happen, but to count on that is naive," Jason Fried explained to me when I asked how he built 37signals, now Basecamp, into a platform with millions of users after pivoting from a Web design company to a Web app company in 2004. "In order for the product to speak for itself, it needs someone to speak to."

As Byrd Leavell, a literary agent, puts it to his clients, "You know what happens if your book gets published and you don't have any way of getting attention for it? *No one buys it*." That can't be what you want!

Al Ries and Jack Trout, likely two of the greatest marketers who've ever lived, acknowledge that CEOs are very busy. They have meetings, phone calls, business dinners, and countless other day-to-day responsibilities. So, naturally, CEOs delegate the marketing to other people. But this is a huge mistake. "If you delegate anything," Ries and Trout say, "you should delegate the chairmanship of the next fund-raising drive. (The vice president of the United States, not the president, attends the state funerals.)" You can cut back on a lot of things as a leader, but the last thing you can ever skimp on is marketing. Your product needs a champion. As Peter Drucker put it: "[Each project] needs somebody who says, 'I am going to make this succeed,' and then goes to work on it."

That must be you. Marketing is your job. It can't be passed on to someone else. There is no magical firm—not even mine—who can take it totally off your hands. Even if you're famous, even if you have a million Twitter followers, even if you have a billion dollars to spend or fancy credentials—it's still on you and it still won't be easy. It's on you to take this great thing you've made and reach as many people as possible with it.

What comes next is applying the same amount of creativity and energy into *marketing* as you put into *making*. Before you despair, I hope you can see that that is empowering. Plenty of people can make great work. Not everyone has the dedication to make it and to *make it work*. Marketing is an opportunity for you to distinguish yourself, to beat out the other talented folks whose entitlement or laziness holds them back.

But how am I supposed to do it? That's the critical question. I get it. Marketing does not come naturally to you (or so you think). You don't have the money to do it right. You don't have the time or the skills. I've heard these protests hundreds of times over from clients, colleagues, and conference attendees.

If you can make the time, I can show you the skills. It's easier than you think—I promise. And I'll tell you one other thing: While marketing is *a* job and it's *your* job, it's also a fun and worthwhile job. You're selling something you believe in, that you're invested in, and that you know people will like. If this was pushing something no one wanted or needed, sticking the responsibility on someone else might make sense. But in this case, why should you let them have all the fun?

The Rule You Can't Forget

When I work on a project—with clients, but particularly with my own writing—I start by acknowledging a blunt but important truth: Nobody cares about what I have made. How could they? *They don't know what it is.* And if they do know, still the average fan cares a lot less than I would like them to care. This too is undeniable—how can they care much about something they haven't experienced the benefits of yet? They haven't spent years living and breathing this thing like you have—not yet anyway.

Accepting your own insignificance might not seem like an inspiring mantra to kick off a marketing campaign, but it makes a big difference. I always prefer to start from a place of reality, not from my own projections and preferences. Humility is clearer-eyed than ego—and that's important because humility always works harder than ego.

I remind myself: People are busy. They have no idea why they should care about this thing. No one is eagerly awaiting it as if it was the sequel to a blockbuster franchise (and even if it is—you're far better off pretending it's not and working just as hard). People have been burned too many times before by other people who didn't take as much pride in their craft as I do. It is my job as the marketer of my work to *make people care*, and that's not going to be possible if I start with any illusions or entitlements. Instead, I'm going to start fresh. I'm going to win my readers, customers, and fans for the first time, one person at a time, all over again.

The only way the job will get done—*to make people care*—is if we do it ourselves.

This is something I've had to tell multimillionaires, celebrities, bestselling artists, and people with millions of YouTube subscribers. I've had too many clients who assured me of their magic bullet—a high-traffic blog, a friend who works for _____, their close relationship with [insert show], their millions of fans—and that because of this they were all set. They blew off opportunities or dismissed great ideas, all because they were too conceited, distracted, or busy to make marketing a priority. Then, a few months later, I'd see them come back to me with the bad news: Their brilliant game changer/disruptive technology/once-in-a-lifetime/sure thing/[insert your own egotistical hyperbole here] launched to crickets.

One client, successful enough to travel by private jet, wanted to appear on a handful of very influential podcasts to promote his first major work in a long time. After securing the placements, I talked him through the scheduling. He interrupted, "I'm busy. Can't I just get them all on the line at once and record all the interviews together?" No, I said. These people aren't here for whatever scraps you're willing to throw them. You may be important in your world, but they are important in theirs. We have to treat them with respect—we have to respect their audiences, just as you respect yours. Thankfully, he agreed to do it right, and we reached several million people with an investment of just a few more hours of time.

Another client had a penchant for brainstorming big, aggressive marketing ideas with his team. But then he never executed any of them, declining to cough up the budget or make the time because everything else seemed to be going well. The book debuted at number two on the list instead of clinching the top spot he'd wanted. The worst part? The narrow miss ate at him, even though it was perfectly avoidable.

What would hustle have gotten him? A few more people who cared. A few more people who were able to learn about his book through the thicket of pings, posts, tweets, shares, and all other manner of digital noise that assaults us each day. It would have gotten him the number-one spot.

A recent study found that when you visit the Facebook News Feed, more than 1,500 pieces of content are vying for your attention. There is, in other words, a 1-in-1,500 chance of even *seeing* a desired customer.

The mark of a future perennial seller is a creator who doesn't believe he is God's gift to the world, but instead thinks he has created something of value and is excited and dedicated to get it out there. Guess what? A sense of entitlement is not how you're going to reach them. Hunger and humility make the difference.

Anything Can Be Marketing

If the bad news is that nobody cares, the good news is that there are lots of ways to *make* them care. There is this great line from venture capitalist Ben Horowitz: "There is no silver bullet. . . . No, we're going to have to use a lot of lead bullets."

Lead bullets might not be futuristic—but they work. A campaign that author Steven Pressfield did in 2011 for his book *The Warrior Ethos* is the perfect illustration. At the time Pressfield was already a successful, world-class writer who'd sold millions of books over a twenty-year career. But this was a book he was self-publishing, which meant he had no big traditional publishing machine to support him.

What did Steven do? He had the idea to pay to print approximately eighteen thousand copies of *The Warrior Ethos* in a special "Military Edition" that was not for sale. Then he gave those copies away through contacts he had in the armed services. Eighteen thousand print copies! That's harder to do than you think: to find all those people, convince them to be an early reader, and deliver the copies to them. The shipping and delivery logistics alone would be a nightmare. (I know—I gave away more than a thousand copies of one of my books to marketing students and it was exhausting!)

In the first month, as the advance copies made their way into readers' hands, the book sold twenty-one hard copies and thirty-seven ebooks. It took five more months until the book sold five hundred copies in a single month. But it was all heading in the right direction. Within five years of publication, the book had sold roughly sixty thousand copies. On Amazon, its rank remains consistently better than ten thousand (it is occasionally number one in various categories) and the book has around 350 reviews. Like an annuity, it sells more than one thousand copies per month, each and every month—thus averaging between twelve thousand and fifteen thousand copies a year. Five years from now, if the Lindy effect holds true, we should see that *The Warrior Ethos* will *still* be selling that many copies.

Is giving the book away by hand to the military really marketing? Sure it is—because ultimately it moved a lot of product. Bonobos, the high-end pants retailer, sold many of its first pairs literally by hand because its founder carried a duffel bag of them with him wherever he went. At a friend's wedding? Check. At a poolside brunch? Check. It worked and got customers, so it's marketing.

Wayne Dyer, whose first book sold some six million copies,

started the same way, peddling the book out of the trunk of his car. *Once a Runner*, the cult classic novel about running by John Parker Jr., got traction in the parking lots of track meets and running events in which Parker was participating. In fact, Nike itself started that way, with Phil Knight selling the shoes himself at track meets out of the back of his Valiant. He'd been rejected from all the local stores, but found that when he spent time actually talking to runners and coaches he "couldn't write orders fast enough." Jay Z sold CDs out of his car before anyone would give him a record deal; so did the founders of Cash Money Records. A founder hustling like a door-to-door salesman? Again, if it works, well, then it's marketing.

Only One Thing Matters: Word of Mouth

Take a second. The album you've listened to a couple of hundred times. The restaurant you visit on every special occasion. The shoes you wear—the style you've bought at least ten pairs of over the years. How did you first get turned on to these perennial sellers in your life? How do you find most of the things you like or consume on a regular basis? How did you find your favorite book of all time?

If you're like most people, it's not from advertising or even from PR. It's because people you listen to, trust, or respect talked to you about it. We discover things by *word of mouth*.

A friend says, "Hey, you should check this out." A mentor tells you about the most influential book or movie in her life. An attractive stranger sits next to you on the train and you ask what kind of backpack he's carrying. He tells you the brand and how much he loves it.

How did I hear about Cyril Connolly some seventy-eight years after *Enemies of Promise* came out and forty years after his death? It certainly wasn't from something set up by his publicist or publisher. Someone I trusted said it was good. Now hopefully the same thing has happened to you. *And so it goes . . .**

These are all organic, natural recommendations of products or ideas—and they are, without question, the single most powerful force in the life of a product. No one has the steam or the resources to actively market something for more than a short period of time, so if a product is going to sell forever, it must have strong word of mouth. It must drive its own adoption. Over the long haul, this is the only thing that lasts.

According to a study by McKinsey, between 20 percent and 50 *percent* of all purchasing decisions happen from some version of word of mouth. And the study found that a "high-impact recommendation"—an emphatic endorsement from a trusted friend, for example—converts at *fifty times* the rate of low-impact word of mouth.

A product that doesn't have word of mouth will eventually cease to exist as far as the general public is concerned. Anything that requires advertising to survive will—on a long enough timeline—cease to be economically feasible. As Jonah Berger, one of the leading scientists on viral sharing, has put it, "[Companies] live or die by word of mouth."† In fact, he found that in some industries, like skin care and phones, word of mouth was *twice* as effective as paid advertising. (And remember, those industries spend *billions* in ads.)

Our marketing efforts, then, should be catalysts for word of

---

* That's a Kurt Vonnegut quote from *Slaughterhouse-Five*, by the way. You should check him out too. Also very good.

† Read Jonah's book *Contagious* as well. (And see *word of mouth*!)

mouth. We are trying to create the spark that leads to a fire. Pardon the environmentally unfriendly analogy here, but with a perennial seller we're not looking for a tidy campfire—we're looking for our version of the Centralia coal mine fire, which has been burning since 1962 and should last another 250 years or so.

Everything that follows in this chapter is a tactic in line with that strategy. As Seth Godin has written, creating successful word of mouth begins with a single customer. "Sell one," he says.

"Find one person who trusts you and sell him a copy. Does he love it? Is he excited about it? Excited enough to tell ten friends because it helps them, not because it helps you? Tribes grow when people recruit other people. That's how ideas spread as well. They don't do it for you, of course. They do it for each other."

So how do you find those first people? How do you bring them in? Well, that's what marketing is about. You have to bring in those first customers, or there will be no friends to tell!

The Launch

With word of mouth as the ultimate goal, the timeline for how we think about marketing shifts a little bit. We have more runway than just opening weekend or the first month of sales. We're able to think long term as we evaluate our campaign. Indeed, many perennial sellers take decades to truly sell—sometimes it's not until their creator dies that the public fully appreciates the work.

From a mythmaking perspective, these stories of eventual success have a certain allure, an "I told you so" karmic justice. For the real human beings who have to live in the real world, though, obscurity is probably less glamorous than we like to pretend it was. Someone once lauded the Southern writer Padgett Powell for never having become a commercial author. Powell's reply was simple and honest: "Nothing to admire."*

I think the point is: There's nothing impressive about *not* breaking through. Building a huge commercial audience is incredibly difficult—and not everyone manages to do it. The strategy of perennial success is about trying to create work and products that will sell over the long term, but ideally we also want to sell in the short term. Put differently: Selling in perpetuity and launching strong are not mutually exclusive.

History shows that good work eventually finds its audience, but, as John Maynard Keynes so accurately expressed it, the market "can remain irrational longer than you can remain solvent." If an artist starves to death before the world comes around to appreciating her genius, is that a good thing? If the writer has to get a day job to pay the bills and that work begins to impede on her ability to do creative work, clearly that's not a positive development. Nor is it an uncommon one. Most of us can't patiently remain undiscovered for very long.

Executing a successful launch—marketing to find our audience immediately instead of resigning ourselves to the great meritocratic arc of the universe—is how we're able to survive, and to build and thrive in our creative career. Great stuff may inevitably find an audience. But who can afford to wait?

Apple's classic products have lines out the door when they launch. Plenty of Hall of Famers set records their first season—sometimes in their debut appearances. Many classic books debuted on the bestseller lists. Why *wouldn't* you want to be a hit right now?

---

* Thanks to my friend Austin Kleon, who pointed me to this and to some of the Springsteen examples in this book as we kicked around this very struggle over lunch one day.

Don't fool yourself by saying, "Oh, I'm playing a long game, so it doesn't matter how I market myself." W. Somerset Maugham observed that while those who ultimately achieve "literary posterity" in the long term may surprise us, the market and history still tend to choose from those who were known in their day. "It may be," he said, "some great masterpiece which deserves immortality has fallen still-born from the press, but posterity will never hear of it." Which is why, as Truman Capote reminds us, "A boy has to hustle his book."* The same goes for whatever you happen to have made. Gotta hustle it.

"People also tend to like things that other people like," Cass Sunstein observed in his fascinating study of how *Star Wars* became the sensation it is. "Whenever there is a big fuss, most of us want to know what it is all about." *That* is the reaction our marketing is aimed to create.

A fuss can develop slowly, but it's more powerful when it's quick and concentrated—and there's no reason not to market in a way that best sets you up for the latter. A proper launch is very much in your control. It's possible for you, without a PR firm, without a big ad budget, to kick off with an artillery barrage of marketing†—that is, press, interviews, news coverage, social media buzz, preorders from your hard-core fans, strong store placement, and everything else. I know it's possible because I've done it and I've helped other people do it too.

---

* At the time, a *Life* columnist, who complained that Truman's marketing made him a "huckster," asked, "Why didn't, wouldn't, couldn't Capote for heaven's sake just shut up?" Well, his book is still selling two thousand copies a week and no one remembers that critic's name.

† I like "artillery barrage" as the analogy; I've also heard it described as the "surround-sound effect." For the launch of *In Cold Blood*, Truman Capote's publisher referred to the author's speeding train of a marketing campaign as the "Capote Special" and admitted that he was driving it and everyone else was a passenger.

James Altucher had written eleven books prior to working with my firm, Brass Check. They're great reads, but none had sold particularly well. With *Choose Yourself*, not only was James open to rigorous editing, he was also open to the idea of trying a proper launch for the first time. In the past, he'd just sort of *released* books but without much in the way of a plan. What we ended up doing with him follows almost every strategy you'll see in detail below, but the biggest change we made was to concentrate all our efforts around a launch window. A lot of creators are like that, especially when they are self-funded or self-published—they just want their thing out in the world. They don't want to wait; they just want to go, go, go.

In order to sell over the long term, we knew the faster we hit critical velocity, the better our chances of making it would be. That meant waiting and it meant coordination. I remember a few occasions talking to James about a potential article he wanted to write or an interview he wanted to do in the run-up to the release. Let's wait, I would tell him. Let's put it out all on the launch date— that's why we have one.

Products used to have a launch date because that was literally the first possible day it would be available in a store—which came almost as a celebration of the end of a long, difficult period of production, shipping, stocking, and all sorts of other manufacturing and retail hurdles. But today, it takes five seconds to get something up and for sale online. That means a launch day is a choice rather than a logistical necessity. You might think that this makes launches less important, but that's not so.

From a marketing perspective, a proper launch is essential— much more than simply picking a random day to go live. Yes, "launch windows" are artificial. But just because something is *constructed*, as I once heard a wise person say, that doesn't mean it isn't important. In fact, the artificial notion of a launch is almost more important now than ever—customers have so much choice, they tend to choose what appears to have momentum. As Sunstein observed, people choose what others are choosing.

James's launch ended up having all sorts of successes, from a highly viewed book trailer to a number of provocative articles to a solid amount of Amazon reviews to multiple podcast appearances to some media stunts and even a big giveaway. All this was tapping into different audiences, all at the same time, to jump-start the word of mouth in all those communities. It was the spark that lit the fire that was the book.

I saved the following tweet from a fan named @SteveCronk fan during the campaign, since it sums up why launches matter:

> Fine, I'll buy your book @jamesaltucher. Now stop being EVERYWHERE ON THE INTERNET like you have the past two weeks

The barrage worked. We wore him down—I don't think that's a bad thing. And, if the book delivered on the promise the marketing had made, positive word of mouth would follow.

Of course, had things gone differently, *Choose Yourself* would likely still have sold well—just not as well and not as soon. Almost all the things James did for the launch, from articles to interviews, would have happened anyway. We got more out of them by concentrating their timing in a small window.

Record labels know that the more times you hear a song, the more likely it is to be a hit. That's why they hold tracks back until they get a number of stations committed to playing it. It's the same thing with the marketing of any product. You're doing a lot of work in advance so that to the public it feels like you're suddenly everywhere.

This requires you not only to give yourself a proper launch point, but enough runway to hit it. The component parts of a launch—media, relationships, influencers, advertising, creating content—all take time and effort. They would take time even if a creator were to do them poorly. To do them right, to line them up right, to coordinate them properly is like a military operation. Do not gamble. Do not rush!

What Do We Have to Work With?

Other than the "when," the most important part of a launch is the "what"—as in: *What are we working with here?* The first thing anyone planning a launch has to do is sit down and take inventory of everything they have at their disposal that might be used to get this product in people's hands. Stuff like:

Relationships (personal, professional, familial, or otherwise)

Media contacts

Research or information from past launches of similar products (what worked, what didn't, what to do, what not to do)

Favors they're owed

Potential advertising budget

Resources or allies ("This blogger is really passionate about [insert some theme or connection related to what you're launching].")

It is essential to take the time to sit down and make a list of everything you have and are willing to bring to bear on the marketing of a project. Aside from racking your own brain, one of my favorite strategies to kick off this process is simply to *ask your world*. I call this the "Call to Arms"—a summons to your fans and friends (see Platform, Part IV of this book) to prepare for action. I typically create a quick online form and I post it on my blog as well as on my personal Facebook page and other social media accounts. In a previous era, different tools would have been used (a physical Rolodex?), just as there will doubtlessly be newer, different tools in the future. Regardless of the tools used, though, what you're saying is the same:

> Hey, as many of you know, I have been working on _____ for a long time. It's a _____ that does _____ for _____. I could really use your help. If you're in the media or have an audience or you have any ideas or connections or assets that might be valuable when I launch this thing, I would be eternally grateful. Just tell me who you are, what you're willing to offer, what it might be good for, and how to be in touch.

Depending on the size of your platform, the number of messages you get might range from a few dozen to a few thousand, but there will almost always be something of use in there.

People are often sitting on assets they haven't bothered to think about and they inevitably trickle out far too late in the process. "Hey, I went to college with [insert important big shot]." "Oh, yeah, [insert reporter] wrote about my company a few years ago." Maybe you have an influential account on a certain social media site. What about all the email contacts you've built over the years? Maybe the newspaper in the town you grew up in loves to write about local success stories—that's an asset, even if you've never spoken with them before. The sooner you know about all these, the sooner you utilize them.

However many of these relationships you have, however tenuous or weak you might feel they are, put them all in a spreadsheet. Lay it all out—names, outlets, promises, debts—and see what you've got to work with. If it's a tiny spreadsheet, that's okay. If that is the case, though, I'd take a minute to consider what this says. Is it that you'll need to go it alone and make up for this lack of resources with extra hustle and intensity? Or would waiting until you're better supplied and prepared make the most sense?

A general wouldn't even think about going into battle without knowing how many troops and weapons and supplies he has. And he certainly wouldn't go into battle if he determined that he didn't have enough of any one of those things to make the difference. Discretion, they say, is the better part of valor.

The other asset you have—that every good product has—is the product itself. If you've actually succeeded in solving a problem (or problems), then what you have in your hands right now is worth a lot to a significant number of people—ideally, to a significant number of many different types of people. When that happens, the product can do double duty at the center of one of the most powerful and counterintuitive marketing strategies I have ever seen.

Free. Free. Free.

Before he was one of the biggest, bestselling rappers in the world, 50 Cent was a crack dealer on the streets of Jamaica, Queens. One of his strategies was to pay his crew to rob rival drug dealers, take their stash, and then give those drugs away for free as samples around the neighborhood. Then, as the only game in town, with a number of clients hooked on his product, he captured the entire market.

Now, we can say that this is abhorrent and violent, and we'd be right. Morality aside, it's also brilliant marketing and sales strategy. A smart business friend once described the art of marketing to me as a matter of "finding your addicts." That's literally what 50 Cent was doing, and figuratively what every creator is attempting to do at launch. Have you *seen* the lines outside an Apple store the week of an iPhone launch? Or the line outside a multiplex the week before a *Star Wars* release? Or the mob outside a Niketown the day the new LeBron James shoe drops? Those people are not bargain shoppers or casual fans. Those are *addicts*.

Ideally, with the work we've done in the first two parts of this book, we've made our books, movies, products, comedy, or artwork as addictive and captivating as they can be. Quality is no longer the issue. Our problem is that most people have *no idea our stuff even exists*. They haven't had a taste yet, so how could they?

The publisher and technologist Tim O'Reilly puts it well: "The problem for most artists isn't piracy, it's obscurity." In other words, we spend a lot of time insisting that nobody steal our work or get it for free . . . but we forget that being *unknown* is a far worse fate for an artist than being underpaid.

How much does the thing you're selling cost? Twenty dollars? Fifty dollars? A thousand dollars? Whatever the price, we typically demand it up front from our customers. But that is not the whole story, nor the full price. In addition to the actual cost, there's also the cost of buyers' time to consume the product—there are all the things they're missing out on by choosing to consume your product (what economists call opportunity costs). I can't ever get the two hours of my life back if the movie isn't good. I can't get a refund on time I've spent listening to your album. Life is short, and we can read only so many books—by choosing one, I'm choosing explicitly to not read another. That weighs heavily on consumers.

There's another cost that creators tend to miss too: How much does it cost for people to find your work? To read the reviews or read an article about it? How much time does it cost to download, wait for it to arrive, or set up? These costs—transaction and discovery costs—exist even when your work is free! Think of the free concerts you haven't attended, the samples you didn't bother to walk over and try, the products you didn't buy even though they were 100 percent risk-free, love it or get your money back, no money down. When you think about it this way, it's really amazing that people buy or try anything at all!

When we say, "Hey, check this out," we're really asking for *a lot* from people. Especially when we are first-time creators. Why should anyone do you this favor? Why should they trust you? Why take the risk? Hugh Howey, author of the wildly popular *Wool* series and one of the first big successes in the self-publishing era, has said that it's essential for debut authors to give away at least some of their material, even if only temporarily. "They've gotta do something to get an audience," he's said. "Free and cheap helps." So does making the entire process as easy and seamless as possible. The more you reduce the cost of consumption, the more people will be likely to try your product. Which means price, distribution, and other variables are not only essential business decisions, they are essential *marketing* decisions.

Tim Ferriss has posed an interesting related question: "If TED charged for their videos from the beginning, where would they be now?" The answer is probably closer to "obscurity" than "ubiquity"—the conference has racked up billions and billions of views since the first videos went up. Why should our work be any different?

Sure, free is an easier strategy for some products than others. The indie musician Derek Vincent Smith (aka Pretty Lights) did this so often and so prolifically, it not only built him a huge audience for live shows but also earned him a Grammy nomination. Starting with his first album in 2006, Pretty Lights has given all eight of his albums and EPs away for free on his website. "I knew I'd probably have to support myself and my music through live performance, so I wanted to get it through as many speakers as possible," he told *Fast Company*.

Starting in 2008, his music was available for paid download on iTunes and Amazon, while still being free for anyone to download from his website. This gave his fans a choice of supporting him financially while still growing his audience through free downloads. By 2014, Smith was averaging, per month, 3,000 paid album downloads, 21,500 single downloads, and three million paid streams on platforms like Spotify. His album *A Color Map of the Sun* was nominated for a Grammy in 2014, after being downloaded free more than a hundred thousand times in its first week of release.

Giving away music for free does not impede sales. I was reminded of this the other day when I was flipping through my music library and came across a couple of albums that I've listened to at least a hundred times over the years. I traced back how I'd first heard them—because they aren't bands I usually listen to—and I remembered: The albums were streamed for free on MTV.com during their launch week. I listened as a high school student, then purchased the physical CD, and now the albums follow me from laptop to laptop, iPhone to iPhone.

To go back to the TED conference for a second, remember: The videos are free to watch online. It still costs close to $10,000 to actually attend the conference and people are dying for tickets. One drives the other.

For books, the free strategy is possible in a variety of iterations. Authors can give away whole chapters, excerpts as articles, or a free preview—or they can give the whole thing away for free to a select audience, or have events or sponsors buy copies that are in turn given away for free. In one form or another, my own books are almost entirely available for free online. If there is good content inside the book, I want to publish it for free online because it's my best sales pitch. My books are often uploaded to pirate sites (you may be reading a pirated copy right now), and I've also done big giveaways in the past. The stories in Tucker Max's *I Hope They Serve Beer in Hell* were all available online—and still are today—but that certainly didn't stop the book from selling over a million and a half copies. If anything, the free stories largely drove those sales. In 1985, the novel *Beaches* (which became a hit movie and even bigger sound track) was launched with a campaign in the *Los Angeles Times* that offered a free copy of the book to the first two thousand people who wrote in. The giveaway also included a copy to give to a friend.

The rapper Soulja Boy launched his career by uploading his own songs to the early pirating platform LimeWire, but he deliberately misnamed the tracks so users thought they were getting free downloads of the latest 50 Cent and Britney Spears singles. Most users would immediately realize the mistake, but others, Soulja thought, might like what they heard. The author Paulo Coelho didn't freak out about piracy—he *actively pirated his own books* on torrent sites in countries like Russia. Why? Because he didn't have a marketing budget and found that it was the fastest and most effective way of driving legitimate sales in those hard-to-reach regions. Coelho sold around ten thousand copies of one of his novels in Russia in one year. The next year—driven largely by the piracy—he sold one hundred thousand (which surely calmed his originally angry publisher). He once posted a photo on Facebook of a young boy selling unlicensed copies of his books in the streets of India. He didn't post the photo to shame the boy but to thank him, writing, "I know that people call this 'pirate' editions. But for me this is an honor, and an honest way for this young man to make money." Coelho has sold an almost unheard-of 165 *million* books; it's a strategy that's clearly working.*

Contrast this with the way traditional publishing, or really any traditional business, operates. They try to eke out every dollar, squeeze every drop of revenue out of whatever they have while in the process ruining their prospects for long-term sales and growth (i.e., brand loyalty). The restaurant I ate breakfast at this morning keeps a pen on a filthy lanyard made of rubber bands at the register so someone won't steal it. My favorite part? It's not even the restaurant's pen—it was clearly stolen from the bank up the street. Meanwhile, the restaurant pays for a big, expensive billboard on the highway to attract attention.

Not long ago, bands like Metallica were *suing* file-sharing sites for pirating their work even though (at least in Metallica's case) they'd built their following through tape trading when radio refused to play thrash metal. Today, smart creators realize that the bigger the audience they can reach with their music, the better. On campaigns in the past, I've partnered with BitTorrent, one of the biggest piracy tools in the world, to give away music and books and other content for precisely this reason.

Aren't these creators worried about losing potential sales? Yes, that is a risk, but it is better than the alternative. Cory Doctorow, a well-known science fiction author and editor of one of the biggest blogs in the world, has explained, "Although it's hard to turn fame into money in the arts, it's impossible to turn obscurity into money in the arts. It doesn't matter how you plan on making your

---

* It's not always easy to get partners on board with such a strategy. But as the saying goes, it's better to beg for forgiveness than ask for permission.

money—selling books or downloads, selling ads, getting sponsorship, getting crowdfunded, getting commissions, licensing to someone else who's figured out how to make money—you won't get the chance unless people have heard of your stuff."

Think about all the stuff out there that you *haven't* checked out—*even though most of it is really cheap*. That's the kind of abundance we enjoy as consumers. There is so much out there that you couldn't possibly consume it all in your lifetime. So we ignore a lot of it, especially the stuff that looks expensive.

Which is why as creators we have to get more comfortable with giving people a taste of our work—or, in some cases, giving *some* people the entire meal for free.* That's how we build an audience and gather momentum.

I think you'll find you're already more comfortable with this idea than you know. Would you charge a reporter if she wanted to try your product? If a celebrity walked into your restaurant, wouldn't you comp his meal? If you heard that a social media star with millions of followers loved your stuff, would you think twice about mailing her a bunch of it?

Our initial audience is just as important. We have to get them hooked somehow, and free is often the best way to do it. Many of the much bigger, much more profit-focused companies have to accept this same uncomfortable fact of modern life too. How many of your friends mooch off somebody else's paid HBO GO or Netflix account?

Forms of cheating like this could easily be shut down, but the

---

* With Robert Greene's *Mastery,* we took a thousand pages of interviews he'd done with famous masters for the book and turned that material into a free supplemental ebook (or a free taste, depending on how you look at it). It was downloaded more than twenty thousand times, made it to number 115 on Amazon, and helped make the paid book a number one *New York Times* bestseller.

providers—especially the savvy ones—usually choose to look the other way. The channels see it as a twist on an established business model known as *freemium*, where you give away a chunk of the product and then create extra awesome features on top of it that people want to pay for. That's the essence of a paywall, when you think about it: You get ten articles from the *New York Times* for free each month, but if you want more, then you have to give them your credit card.

Here are just a few of the services that have hooked me (and probably you too) in a similar fashion: Spotify. Dropcam. Basecamp. Amazon Prime. Some of these were thirty- or ninety-day free trials. Others were introductory versions of more advanced products. Regardless, I was hooked like 50 Cent's early "clients" and now I pay for them—but only because I discovered it for free first.

That doesn't mean that the knee-jerk reaction against piracy is wrong. Metallica was right from a legal perspective—they were just shortsighted (or they were at a point in their career where monetization mattered more than exposure and discovery).

By contrast, humor writer George Ouzounian, also known as Maddox from TheBestPageintheUniverse.com, has given away almost 100 percent of his writing for free—without ads—online for twenty years. Those pieces have been read some five hundred million times in the last decade and a half. When I spoke to him, I mentioned his "free content" and he stepped right in to correct me: "Having content that is free and shareable is an important part of the equation, though it's important to emphasize that it's only free to the reader. My writing costs me a lot to host and maintain because I don't monetize it with ads. I make that clear on my website, so it communicates to the reader two things: 1) that I'm sacrificing for my writing, which means that I write because I have something to say, and 2) I'm sincere with my message.

"Not having ads and fulfilling that promise also builds trust with my audience. That trust is extremely valuable when it comes to my product endorsements, which are few and far between. That's why when I endorse products, services, or people, it's usually extremely successful."

And that's been true not just for the millions of dollars in T-shirts he's sold through his websites, but also for the *New York Times* bestselling (and now perennial-selling) books he's produced and marketed through the site.

If Not Free, Cheap

Earlier I mentioned one of my favorite restaurants in Los Angeles: Clifton's Cafeteria. The venerable downtown dining institution with the tree rising up through the middle of the floor and the neon sign that's been glowing since Franklin Roosevelt was president? It was once a sprawling restaurant chain across Southern California. Its downtown location, Brookdale, featured a waterfall and taxidermy and even a mystic chapel (if that sounds familiar, it might be because it was all mentioned in Jack Kerouac's *On the Road*). Seventy-five years later, the location is still open, having been purchased, remodeled, and updated for a new generation in 2015. As its new owner, Andrew Meieran, reminded us earlier, much of Clifton's success as a cultural institution resides in its sense of timelessness. But I think we can attribute its seven decades of success as a *business* to something else, something simpler: They kept the food cheap. Not only was it cheap, during the Great Depression it had a "pay what you can" policy. As Meieran described it to me, "This fostered a sense of community and belonging that created a very loyal guest base that encouraged generations of repeat customers." Authors like Ray Bradbury and Charles Bukowski were a part of that community—they enjoyed the free lemonade and cheap food while they were poor, and when they became successful, they came back and paid. Bradbury, for his part, celebrated his eighty-ninth birthday there.

Free is a great strategy, but of course it doesn't work in every situation. Traditionally publishing this book, for example, limits my options in that regard. Though I'd be fine giving large numbers of copies away because I'm able to monetize that readership in a variety of ways, my publisher isn't—because it cannot (its business is selling books). Even after giving a lot of books away to drive discovery, at some point I would have to begin to charge, or that discovery wouldn't be worth much. It's quite rare where "free" is a strategy that works indefinitely. This is *business*, after all.

Clifton's found this too. The owner so loved serving people and was so willing to give food away free—slogans included *Dine Free Unless Delighted!* and *You Supply the Party, We Supply the Cake!*—that he nearly went bankrupt. Obviously, that's not going to help anyone. You can't make up a constant per-unit loss simply with volume. Today, Clifton's isn't free. In fact, the new owner put millions of dollars into improving the food and decor so he could charge fair, sustainable prices to keep the business around for another century. Like all things, it's a balance.

The question, then, is: What is the right price to create a perennial seller? This is going to be controversial, but my answer is: *as cheap as possible without damaging the perception of your product.* (And by the way, with the exception of ultra-high-status premium brands, I think damaging the perception of your product through price is very hard to do.)

The reason for this is that a classic of any kind has two characteristics: 1) It's good, and 2) it has been consumed by a lot of people (relatively, at least). One of the best ways to build a readership, viewership, listenership, user base, or customer base early on is by making it cheap.

There's a reason a Wrigley's five-stick pack of gum costs thirty-five cents. "We haven't been the price leader in years," a spokesperson for Wrigley said when the company announced a price increase from twenty-five to thirty cents in 1986, "but when Wrigley raises prices it draws attention." The first Bic pen was priced at nineteen cents. A half century later, it's roughly the same price when you adjust for inflation. Keeping the price low has made it the default pen for millions of people. Instead of running expensive celebrity ad campaigns, Bic's marketing strategy is simply to keep its price low—and that's not an easy thing to do.

Amazon has some pretty great pricing and sales data for books. According to their data, the cheaper a book is, the more copies it sells (and, counterintuitively, makes more money than if it were expensive). Economists call this price elasticity. It's true for almost all products—but it's definitely true when you're launching something. The cheaper it is, the more people will buy it and the easier it will be to market. Yes, there is such a thing as a Veblen good (the more it costs, the more people want it) but more commonly demand is a function of price.

However compelling the math might be, it can still be emotionally difficult to discount our life's work (or at least a big chunk of our life). Selling our work short goes against our DNA as artists. It's hard for people who truly love what they do and value their work highly to accept the realities of commerce. It feels cheap, as if they are insulting themselves. One writer recently told me that she declined to put her book on Amazon—where 70 percent of all book sales come from—because she made more money on each copy selling on her own site. Understandably, she wanted to make as much as she could per sale, but this is not long-term thinking. Any extra revenue she makes per copy is coming at the cost of being in front of only a fraction of her potential audience. That's holding her back from establishing her book as a definitive classic in her space.

The battle against cheap is a long-fought one in the history of publishing. One of the reasons that Raymond Chandler is considered the quintessential noir author is because he embraced the paperback—which other authors and publishers feared would be the death of the industry. His first few novels had sold a few thousand copies each. But with the advent of the pulp paperback— priced at twenty-five cents—Chandler saw those same books immediately sell *hundreds of thousands of copies* (some three hundred thousand for his first novel, *The Big Sleep*, alone),* and then millions in the coming decades. He had reached countless new fans who had previously been priced out of reading. In some cases, they just didn't have bookstores near them, and these new paperbacks were cheap enough for small business owners to carry in their cigar stores, gas stations, or train terminal shops.

Still, many people in publishing thought this was a mistake. They resisted paperbacks, just as they resist cheap ebooks today. They thought it would cheapen the industry and devalue the book. Chandler knew that this was short-term, self-absorbed thinking. In a letter, he laid out logic that applies to just about every craft in the world:

> To these people [in publishing], literature is more or less the central fact of existence. Whereas, to vast numbers of reasonably intelligent people it is an unimportant sideline, a

---

* At a time when the average book sold fewer than twenty-five hundred copies in the United States.

relaxation, an escape, sometimes even a source of inspiration. But they could do without it far more easily than they could do without coffee or whiskey.

Even today, large publishing houses have fought major battles for the ability to determine their own (higher) prices for ebooks on Amazon—and then celebrated when the sales of print books went up. This is moving food around on the plate when they should be focused on bringing more people to the dinner table (i.e., reaching people who otherwise *wouldn't be reading books* in the first place). Chandler's paperbacks were a big, meaty new dish in the middle of the table, made all the more appetizing by the fact that they were specifically pegged to cost less than a pack of cigarettes. If you want to get people's attention, Chandler realized, an effective strategy is to be cheaper and easier than the things they're currently buying and using.

What we've created is a central fact of existence to *us*—after all, we made it. But to most other people, it's optional. They can easily do without our work. A savvy creator embraces this reality and makes taking a chance on it as easy and frictionless as possible for the audience.

I've done a lot of cool marketing campaigns over the years—a few of which have even appeared in lists of the greatest marketing and PR stunts of all time. It is humbling, though, that the single most effective campaign I did for any of my books was discounting *The Obstacle Is the Way*. The publisher reduced the price of the ebook from $9.99 to $3.99 and ran a promotion in a newsletter that specializes in cheap ebooks. Sales more than tripled week over week and stayed steady—so steady that Amazon's algorithm actually kept the discounted price for over a year, effectively subsidizing the cheaper price on my book as a loss leader for their customers. (It's a promotion I've now run several times with other books to great success—including once on Labor Day, when we sold close to five thousand books in twenty-four hours.) Even after the discount ended, sales stayed elevated.* Price *is* marketing.

Are there exceptions to this rule? Of course. As I write this, I am wearing $300 boots from Red Wing, a company that's been manufacturing in the United States for 110 years. Joey Roth's famous teapot, the Sorapot, which I mentioned earlier in this book and which my wife uses many mornings, costs $285. There are plenty of fashion brands that have ruined themselves by discounting their products or distributing through the wrong, cheap retailers. Some things are expensive because if they weren't it would send the wrong message—or their high quality would be impossible at a lower cost. And yet, even in these industries, CEOs will privately express strikingly open-minded attitudes toward counterfeiting and licensing. They know it can serve as an entry point to their product and can market the brand as well.

As a general rule, however, the more accessible you can make your product, the easier it will be to market. You can always raise the price later, *after* you've built an audience.

Find Your Champions— The More Influential, the Better

The story of John Fante is a heartbreaking one. A great novelist's career was partly ruined by Hitler—and the world was deprived of many great books. Yet there is another wrinkle in that story that gives it a somewhat happy ending. Because after fifty years of lan-

---

* More important, getting a single speaking or consulting gig out of the promotion would effectively pay for all the discounting and then some.

guishing in obscurity, *Ask the Dust* was discovered in the Los Angeles Public Library by the writer Charles Bukowski. Bukowski was blown away and began to rave about Fante to everyone he knew—including his editor. What ensued was a resurgence of Fante's work. He spent his dying days finishing one last novel, and today there is a public square in downtown Los Angeles named after him, which isn't bad for a man who was nearly forgotten by history.

I know that I heard about Fante from another one of his fans, the writer Neil Strauss, who in an interview had called *Ask the Dust* his favorite novel. In turn, I have become a champion of Fante and helped sell thousands of copies of his work to my own fans. The power of champions is that they can bring art back from the dead.

It can also breathe first life into something in the way that even the most prestigious or wide-reaching media cannot. I've watched an Instagram post from an influential person take a book to the top of Amazon; meanwhile, a *New York Times* profile about the same project had next to no impact. When a real person, a real human being whom others trust, says "This is good," it has an effect that no brand, no ad, no faceless institution can match.

For nearly twenty years, the single most powerful endorsement in all of stand-up comedy came from Johnny Carson. If a stand-up comic performed on *The Tonight Show* at any point from the late 1970s to the early 1990s, and Johnny gave him the OK sign or, even better, called him over to the couch, that comic's career changed overnight.

Drew Carey was a normal touring stand-up comic when he went on *The Tonight Show* in November 1991, six months before Carson retired. He got called over to the couch, and nothing was ever the same for Carey after that. "Every agency wanted to meet with me—my managers just got slammed with phone calls. The assistant at their office did nothing but answer phones about me for a week," Carey said. "By the end of the year I had a development deal with Disney." In the twenty-five years since that appearance, Carey starred in a self-titled sitcom that ran nine seasons, hosted the American version of *Whose Line Is It Anyway?*, which also lasted nine seasons, and is currently the host of *The Price Is Right*, going on nine years. And it all began with a nod and a call-over from Johnny Carson.

Most endorsements are organic, accidental even. The question is: How do we draw influencers to our work and increase our chances of it happening to us? How do we increase the odds for these accidents?

The first step is the hardest: making something really awesome that exceeds the expectations even of busy, important people with exacting taste. We spent the first half of this book on that idea—and it matters here most of all. There is no fiercer battle for attention than here, with influencers (and no one with higher standards). Charles Bukowski wasn't going to stake his reputation on John Fante if the work wasn't amazing. Johnny Carson wasn't ever going to give a nod to a comic just to be nice. If you don't have what it takes, there's no way to make this strategy work.

But let's say you do. The next part is actually easier than you might expect. Because self-interest is now on your side. Johnny Carson didn't boost Drew Carey's career out of altruism—he *wanted* to discover great new comics. He wanted his show to be a place where the hottest and best talent came and made their mark. Creators often forget that—that influencers are typically hyper-fans (Carson was a comedian; he loved comedy), and their continued success depends on being seen as tastemakers and leaders. Oprah makes money from her famous list of "favorite things"; bloggers often get a cut of affiliate revenue when they link to products they like. If you can make something that will make them look good? There's a real possibility of something happening.

Kathy Sierra, a well-known programmer and game developer, has spoken about needing to consider "your audience's audience" when designing and marketing a product. She says that creators shouldn't be thinking "Does this make me look good?" When they are pitching or producing they should be focusing on making *their audience* look good. Even better, forget the "looking" part—just make them good, period. Or, as Sierra puts it, make them "badasses."

The next step—when you have something that is likely to make an influencer look like a badass, or benefit that person through a recommendation—is the research. I'm often puzzled by the trouble that creators have identifying the influencers in their space. If you're living and breathing the work you do, the answer should come naturally to you. (Ideally, the influencers should be people who *influence you too*.) But if you don't know, it's time to comb the Web and compile dossiers of potential targets. Who seems to have a big following? Who has a reputation as a taste-maker or trendsetter? Who seems to be highly connected or to hold a position of prominence in your industry? Who seems to have a hunger for films, apps, food, or services like yours?

Again, these people don't have to be famous, but they should matter a great deal to the audience you are trying to appeal to. Then comes the tough part: the reaching out.

Making the Ask (And What to Do When You Hear Yes)

What's the best way to ask someone to endorse or share your work? Trick question. The best way is *not* to ask.

Nobody at Ray-Ban asked Don Henley to mention Wayfarers in the song "The Boys of Summer." It just happened. Because the glasses were exactly right for the mood and the message of the song. I can promise you, no one at American Apparel asked Kanye West to rap about us. ("I need more drinks and less lights / And that American Apparel girl in just tights.") But don't let those beautiful, iconic accidents let you think that these things can't be encouraged.

Marc Ecko built his clothing brand Ecko Unltd. into a billion-dollar company and a staple of street wear and music by perfecting what he called the "swag bomb"—a perfectly tailored and targeted package to the person he was trying to impress. His first influencer was a popular New York City DJ named Kool DJ Red Alert. Marc was addicted to his weekly show, which often featured the latest and coolest trends in hip-hop. To get attention for his company, Marc would camp out in Kinko's and *fax in* special drawings he made to Red Alert's station fax machine. Then he started sending airbrushed hats and jackets and T-shirts. He never *asked* for anything—he just made great work and sent it to select influencers he knew might appreciate it. Eventually, he got his first shout-out on the air, and the brand was never the same.

Marc wasn't just sending out random stuff to random people—he knew who mattered and he knew what they liked. When Spike Lee directed the movie *Malcolm X*, Marc "sent him a sweatshirt with a meticulously painted portrait of Malcolm X on it." The sweatshirt took two days of work to make—even though there was no guarantee Spike would even see it. It turned out that Spike loved the gift and sent Marc back a signed letter. Two decades later, Spike Lee and Marc Ecko are *still* working together.

Of course, it'd be great if the president added your book to his summer reading list or Oprah gave you her stamp of approval.

These can be dizzying, life-changing windfalls for creators—and that's why so many people chase them. But the whole reason those lists matter so much is because they don't take solicitations.

There are plenty of other, less exclusive ways to access influencers that will still move the needle. We might not have cultivated Kanye at American Apparel, but I did spend thousands of hours and tens of thousands of dollars cultivating relationships with tastemakers and trendsetters. One of the best ways I found to connect with people was very simple: I'd notice who was already wearing our clothes or wearing similar products. I'd email them to say hello and invite them to the factory and give them personal tours (something other companies couldn't do). I'd send them nice emails and free products. If a celebrity needed something for a tour, we might custom-fabricate it for them and not charge (again, since we had our own factory, we could do something other companies couldn't). I wasn't *asking* them for anything—I was making offers.

Sometimes, if I heard they were struggling financially, I'd buy ads on their website just to help them stay afloat. I wanted to establish a relationship in which, when we had something new, I could send it to them, and if they liked it, they'd share it with their audiences. Much of this content still exists, and it's still selling products today—even though I haven't worked there or even thought about it for years.

Most of these people were bloggers and Internet celebrities that you've probably never heard of. If I hadn't worked in the fashion industry and immersed myself in it, I probably wouldn't have heard of them either. But they drove millions and millions of dollars in sales for the company. I wasn't chasing everyone; I was chasing a select few, predisposed to like our products. And when it was clear that they did—and their audience was responding to the placements—I would dedicate more and more resources to them.

When you find an influencer who likes your product, hold on for dear life. (Send them more stuff than they know what to do with—chances are they have influencer friends!)

Always put yourself in their shoes: How would you feel if everyone wanted a piece of you? How would you feel if you got dozens of emails a day from total strangers trying to trick you into endorsing products, essentially for free? You'd be overwhelmed. Or you'd be jaded. The fact that most creators—especially big companies—just hire PR agencies to do this pitching for them is an opportunity for the DIY creators who don't. Be a person. Be nice. Think relationship first, transaction second.

The only time I've ever explicitly asked an influencer for anything—"Would you post this for me?" or "The book is out next week; we should be able to share?"—I was able to say it the same way I might have asked someone to water my plants while I was out of town. Because we were friends and we do stuff like that for each other.

I've always found that a critical part of attracting influencers is to look for the people who *aren't* besieged by requests. Authors are inundated with requests for blurbs from other authors; meanwhile, generals, academics, and CEOs are asked much more rarely. Who would be better to go after, then? Try to find the people least likely to get a request from someone like you, and approach them first, instead of going where everyone else is going. Be bold and brash and counterintuitive not only in how you create your work, but also in who you use to market it.

A few years ago, startup founders realized that, while venture capitalists were drowning in potential deals, movie stars, athletes, and musicians had just as much money, were not nearly as jaded, and, in fact, being pitched to often appealed to their egos. People like Ashton Kutcher, the rapper Nas, basketball player Carmelo

Anthony, Bono, the stylist Rachel Zoe . . . (After retiring in 2016, Kobe Bryant raised a $100 million fund.) The result was a new breed of celebrity angel investor who was not only easier to get to, but who also brought enormous cachet and reach along with them.

The last part of the successful utilization of influence is how you *use* it. It's great to have important fans and champions, and their willingness to put your work in front of their audience is a huge advantage. But it doesn't end there.

In my experience, the most effective use of influencer attention is not simply in driving people to check you out, but instead as a display of social proof. A blurb on the back of a book isn't bringing new fans to the book; it's there to convince an interested reader, "Hey, this thing is legit." Katz's Deli has photos of the owner with all the celebrities who've eaten there—but they're hanging *inside* the restaurant. It's to reaffirm to the customers: *You're in a special place. Special people eat here.* In the middle of the restaurant there's also a sign hanging from the ceiling that reads, *Where Harry Met Sally . . . Hope You Have What She Had!*

Social proof sells. The perennial seller acquires it by *being legit*, and then comes up with interesting ways to use it to their advantage.

I'll tell a story about social proof that doesn't have anything to do with creative projects, but I think it serves as inspiration. This story was told to me independently by more than one college basketball coach. All of them were in awe of a move pulled by University of Kentucky coach John Calipari. Typically, when a coach is named into the College Basketball Hall of Fame, he gets up to speak for a few minutes, thanking friends, family, and colleagues. In 2015, when Calipari was inducted to the Hall of Fame, ever the brilliant recruiter, he decided to use his speech as an opportunity to make a statement to high school players who were thinking about what team to play for. He invited more than sixty of his former players, many of whom had gone pro, to attend the ceremony and join him onstage (and in many cases, he paid for their flights out of his own pocket). Instead of talking about all his accomplishments, he thanked them and made the speech about them and what they do on the court. The other coaches marveled at the subtle message Calipari was sending: Play for me and you can end up like these guys.

That is the kind of message we want to send to the people we're trying to recruit to our work. We have to look for creative opportunities to do it.

Getting Media Coverage

Except for a few true recluses, creators typically jump at the chance to be in the media. Almost every creator loves media attention. Even the ones who claim to hate the media, I suspect, love their media image as outsiders who are too cool to care. Seeing your name in print, hearing it over the airwaves, seeing it pop up in a Google Alert makes you feel important—and if that wasn't enough, we can justify the ego boost with the fact that a "media tour" is important marketing. Whether we're trying to appear in traditional outlets like magazines and radio or on big podcasts and online platforms, we take for granted that publicity sells products. That's why we hire publicists, give our time away for free (time that could be spent creating) to be interviewed, and jump through every hoop we can to get attention. Media, we tell ourselves, is an investment.

But is it?

In my experience, almost everyone—from brands to artists—*overestimates* the value of traditional PR. Much of the press that people chase is ephemeral and ineffectual, yet expensive and time-consuming to get. It breaks my heart to see people spending $10,000 to $20,000 per month to hire a publicist and dedicating hours and hours of their busy time around their launch trying to meet absurd media deadlines. (Magazines and other outlets considered "long leads" often require *months* of notice.) I once did a radio show that required me to wait on the phone for north of ninety minutes to do a three-minute segment that sold precisely zero books. And then what happens to an interview like this? It disappears. It's like a firework—it looks pretty but ends up being mostly noise and then smoke.

I've seen clients with pieces on the *New York Times* "Most Emailed" list—as viral as you can hope to be on that site—and watched as the Amazon rank for the book hardly budged. I've seen clients on late-night TV and CNN and everywhere else you can think of deliver results that were . . . meh, at least in terms of sales. I was on 20/20 once and watched my Amazon rank *go in the wrong direction.* Think about it this way: Media outlets have trouble getting people to pay for their own product—what makes you so sure they're going to be able to convince their readers and viewers to buy yours?

At one point, things were different. Crazily different, in fact. Try to consider that the media landscape was once so different that publishers could *charge* media outlets for the privilege of running excerpts of their books. Seriously. These were known as serial rights and were once a fairly significant source of revenue for everyone involved.

Robert Louis Stevenson's *The Wrecker* was serialized in *Scribner's Magazine* over twelve months for $15,000 in 1890s dollars. *Scribner's* also bought the serial rights to F. Scott Fitzgerald's *Tender Is the Night* for $10,000, while *Metropolitan Magazine* bought

The Beautiful and Damned for $7,000. *Collier's* magazine bought Sinclair Lewis's *Mantrap* for $42,500. Interestingly enough, the very first three issues of *Playboy* featured excerpts from Ray Bradbury's *Fahrenheit 451* in three parts for $400 (and the deal was negotiated by a young Hugh Hefner himself). In the 1980s, a prepublication version of Tom Wolfe's *The Bonfire of the Vanities* ran in *Rolling Stone* in twenty-seven parts for a whopping $200,000.

During the first Apollo missions, *Life* magazine paid the entire crew of astronauts and their families some $500,000 in 1960s dollars for the right to cover and write about them for the next few years. The only people who get paid for media like that anymore are the Kardashians.

In any case, since customers aren't paying to consume media anymore, media definitely won't pay you or me for letting us be in their pages or on their airwaves. But there's an opportunity here. While other creators waste their time chasing media that doesn't work, there are plenty of PR strategies that do work—and, better yet, are easier and often costless.

But back to the myth: We tend to assume that press is essential to success because very often really good and really popular things get a lot of press. The question is whether press is usually an *effect* of a really good and popular thing or the *cause* of its goodness or popularity. The number of overexposed box office flops most people could name ought to disabuse us of this notion permanently.

In this sense, traditional press is clearly overrated. As I said, there are also other senses where it might be underrated. One of those places is actually a very big deal: credibility and status.

My appearance on *20/20* might not have moved many units for me, but it was certainly a boon for my career. Its logo looks decent on my website—and no one has ever seen it and asked: "But how long was the segment?" They don't even care if it was positive or negative. I could have been on there for one frame and it still would have been helpful. I once got approved for an apartment based on a press clipping,* and I made my wife happy when I got our wedding announcement in the *New York Times*, and that announcement is just as linkable on a Wikipedia page as a full feature. Press is good for stuff like that. A lot of media is like that, it turns out. While the media might not necessarily convince customers, it definitely helps with recruiting investors and employees and impressing other important gatekeepers.

A reality of our culture is that if you or your product has never been covered in the press, there is a risk that people will think you're a nobody. Unless something is brand-new, it's very rare that someone or something is both definitive *and* unknown. That's why press matters and why it is part of most successful marketing plans.

Still, this signaling is worth only so much—and it's rarely worth *more* than other, more effective marketing techniques like discounting or personalized outreach. That they come at so high a cost in time and money is another concern. Would you be better off flying around the country and individually courting the tastemakers in your space? How many copies could you give away for free for what you're paying your publicist? If you weren't distracted by the dream of framing a *New York Times* article about yourself, what other opportunities would you be able to spot and pursue?

I really want you to ask yourself these questions. Not enough people have the discipline and self-awareness to do it.

---

* The press clipping was for a book advance—which I had significantly exaggerated as part of a stunt.

OK, I Still Want to Get Press

I understand where you're coming from—it's very difficult to dissuade anyone from the seductive appeal of publicity (some things we learn only by experience). If you are going to pursue a press-centric strategy, please listen to my advice on this: Start small.

NBC Nightly News is probably not the first outlet to pitch, and it's not the one you're most likely to succeed with. Instead, you will have more success with PR if you treat it the same way you treated your product design: Identify your core audience and start there.

In 2014, I started getting emails from coaches in professional sports telling me that they'd read my book *The Obstacle Is the Way* and that it was helping their teams win. I had a hazy vision of what this might one day mean: Wouldn't it be amazing if *Sports Illustrated* or ESPN did a piece about how my book was a cult sensation in football, basketball, and baseball? I'd seen it happen for other authors, so I knew it was possible. It was also a long reach for me at that point, however much I might have wanted it. What I did next mattered, but first I'll tell you what I *didn't* do: I didn't immediately call up those outlets and beg them to anoint me with a trend piece.

Instead, I responded to those coaches by offering them as many free books as they wanted. I reached out to other coaches who I'd heard might have been reading it and offered to send more. If I saw a player tweet about the book, I direct-messaged him and offered to send some to his teammates. My publisher and I must have sent hundreds of copies over the next year to athletes, coaches, and managers as the news made its way through the sports grapevine that all they had to do if they wanted copies of my book was to ask for them. Then a friend of mine who works in sports broadcasting asked if I wanted to appear as a guest on a podcast she was doing for a small show in Minneapolis. I said yes, and on the episode we talked about the book's influence on the New England Patriots, one of the teams that had emailed me. This episode made its way to a small fan blog that covered the Patriots, and when they wrote about it I worked hard to have everyone in my network share and comment on the piece. Finally, nearly two years after the journey began, I pitched the story to *Sports Illustrated* and they were into it. That article—"How a Book on Stoicism Became Wildly Popular at Every Level of the NFL"—sold so many books that the publisher ran out of copies for nearly a month.

The way I describe this process is "trading up the chain." In an interconnected media age, outlets pick up and re-report on each other's stories. By starting with a small podcast where I could tell the story on my own terms, which led to a pickup on a small site that covers a niche, and then sharing and spreading that piece so it was seen by the right people, I was able to ultimately go from a tiny show to one of the biggest and most influential outlets in the world. Even without that big payoff, this was a great success—because it was selling books along the way, first to the loyal fans of the podcast and then to die-hard Pats fans. No publicist required.

When my company works with musicians, we start by finding the most obscure and specific outlets you can think of. That's how we get buzz going—we want to create the appearance that interest is bubbling up organically (which, because of our approach, it is). We know that these sites feed into the bigger ones, which feed into bigger ones still. The hard work there is finding the influencers of the influencers—and that can be done only with real research by people who actually care about the market they are trying to penetrate.

This is a far different and far more accessible strategy than vainly (and I mean that in both senses of the word) hoping that

Vanity Fair will decide to do a feature on you because you're just so smart and fancy. This requires more dedication and patience than sending out scheduled press releases and hoping to get lucky. Besides that, it *works*.

The other upside is that it adds an element of *momentum* to your narrative. Where far too many projects experience a flash of publicity and popularity only to disappear under the pressure and expectations of that attention, the steady drumbeat is better. The last thing you want is to get a large hit and for viewers to feel like there is *less* to the story the more they dig in.

The angel investor, former TechCrunch reporter, and partner at Google Ventures M. G. Siegler actually advises startups to avoid angling to be featured or highlighted by Apple in the App Store for this reason (arguably the ultimate editorial placement for apps). Sure, it seems like getting the Apple bump would be amazing, but that isn't always the case.

What you don't often hear about is the flipside: When Apple does bestow a coveted featured spot upon your app, you get to rise above the noise, but the result of that is a lot of noisy would-be users . . . The masses may not be asses, but they can be fickle.

It's better, he says, to start with smaller media and smaller features, then work your way up to the big score. I agree.

It's About Grabbing *Attention, Not Getting It*

Let's say you really are ready to court major media attention and that you're not doing it as some self-indulgent distraction. The good news is that the strategy is actually easier to execute than most people think.

What many creators fail to realize—and it becomes clear only when you've spoken to many reporters over a long period of time—

is that the media is *desperate* for material. Reporters sit around all day hoping to find good stuff, anxious to beat their (many) competitors in getting to it. In this way, the modern media is really a seller's market. Reporters *want* stuff. Their bosses *expect* them to jump on leads that fall in their laps, because they *need* them to publish a lot more than they ever have before. They *crave* page views. In fact, if they don't get page views, they'll soon be out of a job. If writing about you or covering your work in some way gets them what they want (i.e., readers), they're not doing you a favor by covering you. On the contrary, you're doing *them* the favor.

And yet, hungry as they are for fresh stories, these reporters are incredibly busy, underpaid, and besieged with requests from other people who want the same attention you're seeking. While none of them has ever said "Man, there's just too much great stuff out there. I can't cover it all," they rightfully become jaded after the four millionth press release announcing the release of some revolutionary product with a dumb name. Writing about you and your supercool, awesome masterpiece might be good for them, but they don't know it yet. It's on you to take up the burden of explaining to them—rather, *showing* them—why.

At the most basic level, my only strategy for finding and getting media is straightforward. I google reporters' names to find their email addresses and phone numbers (yes, they're publicly available). Then I reach out and explain what I'm doing or what I've done. I let the work and the fact that it matches what they cover—that it's interesting and compelling, and likely to do well for them—do most of the talking for me. (I don't assume it should be interesting to them because it's interesting to me. I make it interesting, period.) There's no real trick to it other than that. Nor does there need to be. If there is a secret to media, it is in the work you've made—in the risks you take and the things you do.

When you have this understanding, press is far easier (and cheaper) to get than you think. I remember one client, Jerry DeWitt, who had been a Pentecostal minister for twenty-eight years. After reading the work of and meeting Richard Dawkins, he eventually became an atheist and, as a result, lost everything and was ostracized by his family and friends. He wrote a deeply moving and inspiring book called *Hope After Faith* documenting his experience. As we struggled to come up with ways to get attention for the book—as well as for his important ideas—Jerry threw out the idea of one day hosting a "church service" for atheists. We ultimately encouraged him to host that service in the Deep South during the week of his book's launch. As it was being coordinated, I happened to have lunch with a friend in New Orleans who occasionally freelanced for the *New York Times*. I mentioned what was happening. The next day he emailed: Please, could he attend and would we mind if he wrote about it for the *Times*? CNN made the same request.

That's what happens when preparation meets relationships meets opportunity. Asking a reporter in New York City simply to write about some new book that was coming out (or the rising trend of atheism) would likely not have worked. But when someone who is writing a book and is an embodiment of that trend does something as provocative and unusual as hosting an atheist church service in the Bible Belt? The most important outlets in the world *ask* if they can write about you. They ask *your* permission.

It can be even better than that. Sometimes they ask *you* to write about it yourself. My company came up with a cool idea for the band Zeds Dead—a popular Canadian EDM duo—in which we equipped some of their fans with heart rate monitors during a concert. (I'd gotten the idea when I saw a viral news story of a woman who posted her Fitbit data after wearing the device during sex.) Knowing that the media might be interested in similar stories, we had a data visualization artist plot out the different heart rates of the different fans at the show in a cool way. How did their heart rates rise and fall with the music? Which songs had the biggest effect? Why was that one guy's heart rate absurdly higher than everyone else's? (He was on drugs.) I pitched it to a friend at Boing Boing, one of the biggest blogs in the world, which had covered the first story. He wasn't interested in writing about it. Instead, he asked us if the band wanted to publish a first-person piece on the experience themselves. Even better.

One of my clients launched his book into outer space. (We got this idea after James Patterson helped a fan blow up a copy of his book.) One music client leaked highly anticipated tracks in the "Missed Connections" section of Craigslist. Another hosted an acoustic concert exclusively for the puppies in the parvo ward of an animal shelter during South by Southwest (we called it "South by South *Woof*"). It had the human audience watching behind the glass in tears. Another time we helped someone release an entire album on what is known as the "dark net"—where criminals go to buy drugs, machine guns, and other terrible things online. I've even worked with a client who encouraged a national boycott . . . of himself!

What all these stories have in common is that instead of hoping—or pitching, a more active form of hoping—that the media would cover these wonderful folks for their intrinsic merits and worth, they took matters into their own hands. They did things that created media opportunities for reporters. They did something that broke through the noise, that made a statement, and they did most of the legwork to boot. The sizzle sold the steak.

But what makes something interesting? What makes for something newsworthy? Those are the essential questions for which I'll give you an easy answer: The most newsworthy thing to do is usually the one you're most afraid of. The thing you joke, "But of course, we can't do that." (One of my most famous stunts began with those exact words.) And then *you have to actually do it.*

Just as Casey Neistat chastened would-be creators about the worthlessness of their ideas compared with their execution, no one gets coverage for *thinking* about maybe doing something. You get coverage for taking a stand, for risking something, for going out there and creating news where there wasn't any before. You don't get coverage for what you feel or what you believe. Only what you do with those beliefs or feelings. During the 2016 election, I didn't sit in my house hoping that someone in the media would ask me my opinion about the candidates. I wrote an open letter to my father titled "Dear Dad, Please Don't Vote For Donald Trump." It just so happened that the Trump campaign got one outlet to *refuse* to print my letter, and a media controversy erupted. More than one million people eventually read the letter as a result, and I got emails from a number of influential people who I didn't even know were reading my writing. The best part? NPR called to talk to me too—the same NPR who we'd pitched unsuccessfully about my recent book. With the letter in hand, they were suddenly much more interested.

I bring all these stories up not to brag but to encourage you—and to assuage any fears you might have. There's no reason to be intimidated by the big media machine. You can make it work for you. Don't be afraid of pissing people off either. I've made a lot of people mad over the years—I've been through it all, and it's not as bad as you'd think. It can actually be fun, as long as what you're doing is consistent with the principles of your work. So create a stir. Make some noise. With the timeline we're considering—years and years of relevance—in the end no one will remember being "offended" by something. The world will just remember having heard about it in the first place.

Now, whether this press you get for your work at launch will drive significant sales is a different matter. Sometimes it will, but oftentimes it won't—at least not by itself. Press hits are often worthless by themselves. As a part of a larger campaign, though, they can be helpful. Still, that is never the point of getting press. The real goal is establishing a presence or building a reputation and profile. Publicity is about temporarily breaking through the noise—if only for a single news cycle—and contributing to the word of mouth that a product eventually needs to succeed.

The Art of Newsjacking: Making It All About You

What if you can't think of an interesting stunt to pull? There is another way to attract earned media: a technique called "newsjacking," popularized by the marketing thinker David Meerman Scott. He defines the concept as "the process by which you inject your ideas or angles into breaking news, in real time, in order to generate media coverage for yourself or your business."

In my experience, the breaking-news element is important but not essential. Trends and popular themes are also powerful forces to piggyback on. A broader definition of "newsjacking" would then be: when people and the media are all talking about a certain topic, insert yourself into that conversation by connecting what you do with what they're already talking about.

A clever example: As a new and novel innovation, drones quickly became a massive media trend. The word inside the newsrooms was that drone stories were traffic gold. This was obviously on Amazon's mind when, on the eve of Cyber Monday—one of the biggest online shopping days of the year—it made a commercial that showed its drone delivery system dropping off Amazon-branded packages on doorsteps across America. Here's the thing: This drone delivery system did not exist. Even as I write this, *it still does not exist*. But that was never the point. Amazon was hijacking the news to its advantage. Everyone went along with it—including *60 Minutes*, where the commercial debuted—because the company had done it so well.

Not every newsjacking attempt needs to happen at such a grand scale. One of the things we did when James Altucher launched *Choose Yourself* was announce that James was accepting Bitcoin payments for the book. He was one of the first authors to do it, and so he got press because outlets and the public were desperate for any bit of Bitcoin news they could find.* Later, 50 Cent did the same thing with one of his albums. Both of them ended up getting media attention, mostly from outlets that don't otherwise cover rap music or books.

Robert Greene and I were also the first authors to annotate excerpts from our books on Rap Genius, a controversial site that was popular fodder for many blogs. At the time, the result was just a little bit of press. But then the site got bigger and bigger, eventually changing its name to Genius.com and attracting millions of visitors. When a couple of years later a book industry site run by *Adweek* wrongly reported that another author was the first to put up an excerpt there, a quick email to the reporter got us mentioned again. Newsjacking again.

Another good example: Every day Google puts up a new home

---

* James had about ten readers actually take him up on it, but it got him on CNBC to talk about that *and* the book itself. This certainly moved a lot more units.

page doodle inspired by some current event, holiday, or famous person. Some are more popular than others, but almost every single one gets some sort of media attention because it connects to some conversation that some group is currently having. Google is able to newsjack the birthday of Nelson Mandela or the anniversary of the first man in space or the celebration of St. Patrick's Day. The result is clean, easy, glowing media attention. Even for a multibillion-dollar brand, that's valuable. It also goes to show that there is *always* something to newsjack, no matter who you are or what you make.

Jane Friedman, the founder of Open Road, told me that her marketing team loves to utilize "months." If they have a classic novel about depression, they take advantage of National Depression Month to get attention and coverage. If they have a memoir of a civil rights leader, then their machine springs into action for Black History Month, and so on and so on.* Your average customer might not know that it is International Women's Day, but it makes for a good hook for a project aimed at mothers on CNN. Same for National Burrito Day or National Lipstick Day, Pi Day (3/14), International Coffee Day, Abraham Lincoln's birthday, the 150th anniversary of the invention of the bicycle, and every other pseudo-important day you can think of.

Fundamentally, newsjacking provides something for media and customers to grab on to. "Oh, I've heard of _____. I'll check out this thing *about* that." When a work of art is inspired by, related to, or a response to something news outlets have already covered, that gives them an excuse to cover it again. It allows them to talk about something unusual, or different from what they typ-

---

* After the popularity of the viral video series "Mean Tweets," Open Road newsjacked it by creating its own spoof—"Mean Reviews"—in which its authors read some of the most cruel and harsh online reviews they had received.

ically see each day. When a customer is watching the news and sees a feature about your project—having been inundated with messages around that theme all day—he or she is more likely to take a chance and pick your stuff up.

The Art of Paid Media

Marketing "experts" call stunts and newsjacking "earned media" because they aren't paid for but are generated the old-fashioned way: by busting your ass to make it happen. The other kind of media—advertising, sponsorships, endorsements—is called "paid media" because, well, you pay for it.

Paid media isn't possible for every project, for a few reasons. The most common is that we don't always have money, and if we do happen to have an advertising budget, we always think it's too small. Advertising just seems so natural: We have this great thing we just slaved away at making; surely paying to put it in front of people will help it sell.

But does any of that logic actually hold up?

First off, some of the most successful products of all time got by with almost no advertising or paid in-store merchandizing. Their success was organic and driven by word of mouth—both of which are free. Second, can you honestly say you've purchased (m)any of your favorite products *because* of their advertising? If you can, let me ask you: Did you *discover* that product through advertising? Or was the ad just a reminder for something you were pretty much already sure you liked or needed?

I've bought quite a lot of it over the years (at least $20 million worth on behalf of clients), but as an effective tool for the *launch* of a product, advertising almost never works. It's far more effective when there is already a considerable audience or sales track record.

There is a terrific exchange between the great editor Maxwell Perkins—who edited F. Scott Fitzgerald and Ernest Hemingway, among others—and one of his authors. The author was complaining that one of his books wasn't getting enough advertising support from the publisher. Perkins's reply—over eighty years old—is still critically relevant to every type of creative. Comparing advertising a product to a man attempting to move a car, Perkins wrote:

> If he can get it to move, the more he pushes the faster it will move and the more easily. But if he cannot get it to move, he can push till he drops dead and it will stand still.*

The same goes for paid in-store merchandizing. In retail, this is called co-op, where businesses pay to get better shelf placement: the front table at Barnes and Noble, a special display at Walmart, being "featured" or paired with other better-selling products on Amazon.com, the lady giving out samples or doing a demonstration at Costco. There's no question these things draw eyeballs, and they certainly don't *hurt* sales. The reality is that very rarely do they function well for *launching* a product or for driving sales unless there is already a substantial base of interest or awareness.

A 1985 *New York Times* article on how publishers create bestsellers describes a similar phenomenon. "If a book is a flop, publishers say, not even a fortune can turn it into a best seller." The article goes on to tell the cautionary tale of a businessman who spent $2 million of his own money to promote a book he'd written

---

* There is also an exchange about advertising between the writer H. L. Mencken and his publisher. Mencken pushed the publisher to include sales numbers instead of reviews in his ad copy, absolutely nailing how marketing works in the process: "Americans always want to do what everyone else is doing. If we could spread the impression that the book is a success, it might really become one."

about a supposed breakthrough drug called phenytoin. More than thirty years after the book's publication, it has eleven reviews on Amazon and his strange campaign has been almost entirely forgotten. In addition to the book, he spent something like $70 million promoting phenytoin as a treatment for depression, which, suffice to say, was not successful. Advertising can add fuel to a fire, but rarely is it sufficient to start one.

A rational, efficient advertising campaign involves two key things: knowing how much a customer is worth to you (or a customer's LTV—lifetime value) and knowing how much it will cost to acquire that customer via the advertising you intend to use (or CPA—cost per acquisition). When ego is stripped from the equation—"I like seeing that billboard of myself on the way to the office each morning"—all that remains is whether the math works. Does this Facebook ad drive sales in a revenue-positive fashion? Are we sure that this TV commercial is driving sales, and at what cost? How many ads can we run until we start to see diminishing returns?

The other reason that advertising isn't an option for a lot of projects is that the real data required to answer the above questions is rarely available when launching something new. Yet time and time again I see clients try to start their project's growth this way—probably because it feels easier than the blocking and tackling discussed elsewhere in this section. Or they want to dive in to some exciting, bold, and *expensive* advertising campaign instead of starting with a small test to see whether it actually works.

Meanwhile, there are plenty of easier things they haven't done or don't want to do that would produce results right now. Taking time off work or hiring a babysitter so you can write fifty personally crafted emails—that's hard and unsexy. Paying for a plane ticket and a hotel so you can give a talk at a major nonprofit—

that's time and resource intensive. Joining a group or a cause to build relationships you can draw on later—hard, unsexy, and difficult to quantify. Spending serious money to create samples and give them away to targeted audiences? That's hard and, understandably, feels like the *opposite* of selling. Working on improving your product until it screams "Share me with everyone you know"—that's less fun than buying a back-page ad that everyone (who still reads newspapers) will see.

Most people wish they could just cut a check and be done with it. They'd like to see the tangible results of their promotion in newsprint on the morning of launch day. I've felt those same impulses—paying for media always seems easier than earning it—but they are worth resisting. Save your money.

Ian Fleming, the commercially minded creator of the James Bond franchise, advised his publisher to advertise for his books after they'd begun to sell well, not only offering to share the costs (£60 for every £140 the publisher put in) but even submitting some of his own ad copy:

> Ian Fleming has written 4 books in 4 years. They have sold over one million copies in the English language. They have been translated into a dozen languages, including Chinese and URDU.
> No. 5 is called FROM RUSSIA WITH LOVE.

Makes you want to buy it, no?

The Koss Corporation has been manufacturing high-end audio equipment and headphones in Milwaukee, Wisconsin, since 1958. In 1972, it paid to advertise on a billboard erected just before the highway off-ramp to its headquarters on the north edge of the city. There has been a Koss advertisement on that billboard every day since—going on forty-five years. Koss's primary goal is not to get customers to veer off the highway right then and there to buy a pair of headphones. As the Koss PR coordinator told a local reporter back in 2010, "We do sell our products right here . . . [but] it's a nice reminder that we're located here." It's a message to the community and the state that, unlike other electronics companies, it didn't ship its operations off to the third world to save some money. There's also a reason the company's billboard ads have never showcased a price: That's not the point.

We would all do well if we had the discipline and awareness to hold off on advertising until we had the material to pull off a campaign as compelling as that. We are better off taking the money set aside for advertising and putting it into every other marketing bucket instead. When the product has real revenue and traction and can fund its own advertising? That's when it starts to make sense.

The only advertising the publisher did for *The Obstacle Is the Way*—now approaching two hundred thousand copies sold—was to support the *Sports Illustrated* article, which showed the book's popularity in sports. We took this amazing piece of PR and made sure tens of thousands of additional people read it through sponsored posts on Facebook and other platforms. And we did that only after we were able to see that the article was converting readers into buyers. Effectiveness was our metric, not existence.

But maybe you do have some money to burn. In which case, here's a crazy idea: Actually put it in a giant pile and burn it, then post the video online. Title it "Here's What We Did with Our Advertising Budget." Or give the money to an orphanage and track the impact of your donation on these children on your website for the next decade. Watch how much attention *that* gets. When you do something unexpected or surprising, it almost always does better than going dollar for dollar against advertisers, who spend millions of dollars a year like it's nothing (because to them it *is* nothing—they're not spending their own money the way you are).

There is one form of underrated advertising that I do like if you have a small budget and want to make a statement. It's the kind done exclusively for the sake of getting publicity and attention—not to convert directly into sales (*Go buy this right now!*). In 2011, the outdoor clothing company Patagonia launched its "Common Threads Initiative" with a full-page print ad in the *New York Times* on Black Friday, featuring the headline "Don't Buy This Jacket." What do you think it was doing? Clearly it wasn't trying to sell jackets on one of the busiest shopping weekends of the year in America. Patagonia was trying to make a point about the quality and durability of its products and show that it wasn't just another fast-fashion company trying to sell you new products every single season—and thus sell more jackets—to the detriment of the environment. Yet, as a *New Yorker* profile on the company's "anti-growth strategy" put it a few years later, in 2015, " 'Don't Buy This Jacket' translated, for many, into 'Buy This Jacket' in 2012."

Creative advertising is probably the least competitive sector of advertising, because most brands either aren't creative or are afraid to be. If you had a billboard in Times Square with a picture of the cover of your book, it might make you feel great, but it wouldn't move the needle.

I have a little personal experience in this regard: After I did an interview with NASDAQ in 2016, they featured the cover of my book *Ego Is the Enemy* on their six-story billboard in Times Square for a few minutes as a thank-you. I got a great picture of it—and my parents thought it was awesome—but as I scanned the crowd around me, you know what I saw? *Complete and total indifference.* Even though there were thousands of people around,

I didn't see a single one of them look up. When the ad disappeared, the only thing that remained was my fleeting memory and a pretty cool Facebook post. I certainly didn't see a sales spike.

Newsjacking and advertising can intersect as well. At American Apparel, we once got word that a college student in Wisconsin had been attacked while wearing one of our "Legalize Gay" T-shirts. Springing into action, we bought the back page of the school newspaper and ran a large "Legalize Gay" ad condemning the attack and supporting the students. We offered a free T-shirt to any student on campus—to be picked up at the LGBT center on campus. It was advertising that got attention, that gave a special product directly to future customers, *and* that was the right thing to do.

If I were spending my own money on a billboard—let's say for my marketing company—I probably wouldn't mortgage my house to afford whatever ghastly amount it costs to advertise in Times Square. What I might do instead is buy a small billboard in the town where I grew up that said "Dear Teachers of Granite Bay High School, Thanks for Not Believing in Me. Look at Me Now." It's the kind of thing that would get picked up in the local press and then online and people would talk about it forever. Especially if a "concerned citizen"—*nudge, nudge*—took a photo and sent it to a handful of media outlets the day it went up. You'd be surprised how far "a concerned citizen" can get letting a local paper know "about an outlandish, offensive billboard that made my daughter cry."* Anyway, that's just an idea—I haven't actually done that, but I might!

---

* I brainstormed an ad with Neil Strauss when he wrote a book that was in some ways a repudiation of his reputation as a ladies' man and a schemer. On an enormous billboard on Sunset Boulevard, right in front of the CNN building, Neil put up: "ON BEHALF OF ALL MEN, I APOLOGIZE."

Another recent example from our friend Paulo Coelho: With the help of his Brazilian publisher, Coelho ran a series of print and outdoor ads that featured the *entire text* of his famous novel *The Alchemist*. It's a giant block of text in 4.1-point font, so it's basically impossible to read, but it's still a stunningly clever and brazen move. The brilliant ad reads in part, "Thanks to the 70 million who read the book. If you are not one of them, read this ad." The result was immediate coverage in outlets like *Adweek* and, of course, much love on social media.

Even if these ads don't immediately drive a ton of sales, at least they are fun or mean something. And that's a useful way to think about advertising in general: So much of what the public-facing advertising companies do is, inevitably and unfortunately, about stroking their own egos, so why not have a good time while they are doing it? The fact is, humor and levity will probably do more for your brand over the long term than trying to beat people over the head with brilliantly effective advertising copy. So if you are going to advertise—if you have determined that it is wiser to spend a dollar there than on anything else you might do—then at least make sure you have a good time and that your audience has one too.

One Last Thing

When you got to this section of the book, you may have been expecting some special hack or secret sauce for marketing your projects. I'm not saying there aren't any hacks, but they are less important than you think.

I have left out descriptions of how to optimize for different social media platforms for a reason. As I put the finishing touches on this book, Instagram launched its "Stories" feature as a direct

assault on the hockey stick growth of its newer rival, Snapchat.*
Imagine if I spent an entire section on specific tactics for either
platform and the other one ended up winning the arms race to
photo- and video-sharing dominance. Platforms come and go like
the wind. It's always better to focus on the bigger picture, on the
things that don't change.

There's a great exchange involving the philosopher Epictetus
that encapsulates my approach to thinking about marketing. "Tell
me what to do!" the student says. Epictetus corrects him, "It would
be better to say, 'Make my mind adaptable to any circumstances.'"
It is true for marketing, just as it is for life. Principles are better
than instructions and "hacks." We can figure out the specifics
later—but only if we learn the right way to approach them.

When it comes to creating a perennial seller, the principle to
never lose sight of is simple: Create word of mouth. The marketer
of a movie that needs to open big at the box office its first weekend
or the fashion marketer who needs to sell the latest fall trend? They
need hype. They have to spend. The marketer trying to sell knock-
offs or crummy products? They can rely on scammy sales tactics.

A perennial product requires perennial marketing. Yes, we
want to start off strong—but we need to *stay* strong. For this reason, our efforts need to be lean. We can't rely on a silver bullet—
we need a cache of lead bullets. Which is why if you have to choose
between spending money to pay for a publicist or buying your own
products and giving them away to the right early adopters, you
should go with the latter every time. One is a direct route to word
of mouth; the other is a detour and depends on being at the right
place at the right time in the right news cycle.

---

* And since I wrote this sentence, Snapchat changed its name simply to Snap.
Trying to stay "current" is an absurd race.

In the end, the freemium model, crazy stunts and newsjacking, or being provocative for provocation's sake are just tools. In my experience, these strategies are powerful tools but your project may not need them. Maybe your project is just brilliant and perfectly timed enough that media will flock to you without effort and the press will be fawning and consistent. Maybe the influencers will embrace you without any work on your end. Maybe none of these things will work at first, but after a couple of starts and stops they will.

The best strategy is to try everything and see what works for your project—because it's going to be different for every single project. When you find something, stick with it. Marketing is the art of allocating resources—sending more power to the wheels that are getting traction, sending it away from the ones that are spinning. And investing in each strategy until the results stop working. Then find the next one!

Part IV

PLATFORM

From Fans to Friends and a Full-Fledged Career

I had acquired what, to my mind, is the most valuable success a writer can have—a faithful following, a reliable group of readers who looked forward to every new book and bought it, who trusted me, and whose trust I must not disappoint.

—Stefan Zweig

At a certain point in every project, our marketing and promotional efforts hit a point of diminishing returns. Sales slow, the newness fades, and, if we've done our job properly, word of mouth seems to be carrying on just as effectively without marketing support as it does with it. Sure, as the creator you could go on hustling—but would that be the best use of your time? It is here that we must turn away from the work into which we've just thrown everything we have and focus on two new priorities: ourselves and our *next work*.

Becoming a perennial seller requires more than just releasing a project into the world. It requires the development of a *career*. It means building a fan base both before and after a project, and it means thinking differently than most people out there selling something.

My inspiration in publishing wasn't the authors at the top of the bestseller lists, and it wasn't rappers decked out in chains with fleets of expensive cars. My inspiration was a band from the eighties that many people, to their detriment, have forgotten. I'm talking about heavy metal legends Iron Maiden.

Since 1975—that's *forty* years and counting!—Iron Maiden has defied every stereotype, every trend, every bit of conventional wisdom about not just their genre of heavy metal but the music business as a whole.

Just look at this list of accomplishments:

- 16 studio albums
- 11 live albums
- 24 world tours
- 2,000 concerts in 59 countries
- Over 90 million albums sold
- 5 number one albums
- 42 singles
- 15 million combined social media followers
- Over 200 million views on YouTube

Iron Maiden performed for 250,000 people as the headliners of the Rock in Rio festival—*twenty-six years after the band was formed*. They sell their own beer, they are one of the highest-earning acts in the world, and they travel from sold-out stadium to sold-out stadium in a Boeing 757 *piloted by the lead singer*, often shuttling loyal fans and crew along for the ride. Is that not a model for every aspiring perennial creator?

What's most impressive about Iron Maiden is *how* they achieved all this. This didn't just happen, you know. It wasn't built on the back of one hit album or one giant single. This is a band that was hardly *ever* played on the radio—and certainly hasn't been for decades. This is a band that plays ten-minute songs about science fiction novels and historical figures like Genghis Khan and Alexander the Great. This is a band with *three* guitarists who each get a solo on each song. I mean, the name "Iron Maiden" itself comes from a medieval torture device, for Christ's sake.

No, it took decades of work for Iron Maiden to reach the heights they currently enjoy. It meant thinking not only of creating one perennial seller, but of applying that mindset to everything they did. What's most inspiring to me is that, despite the fact that a huge portion of the population probably has no idea that they're still a band—and swaths of a generation has never heard of them—the band doesn't care. They care about their fans and their fans only. Those are the only people they talk to, the people inside what we are going to talk about in this chapter: *their platform.*

Where other bands relied on radio, on being on MTV, on being timely or on trend, Iron Maiden focused on one thing and one thing only: building a cross-generational global army of loyal fans who buy every single thing they put out. Other acts are dependent on promotion—PR, advertising, store distribution, artist collaborations, and big-budget music videos—to stay relevant and reach an audience, but Iron Maiden cultivated a direct and intimate connection with their fans that allows them to skip those tricks. The result is that the band is *killing* it.

I confess to a small bit of bias here: I've been a die-hard Iron

Maiden fan since I first (accidentally) pirated one of their songs in 2001.* Since then, I've seen them live three times, bought countless albums, a box set, a live DVD, three T-shirts, two belt buckles, streamed a documentary, and God knows what else.

There is a theory by Kevin Kelly, the founder of *Wired* magazine. He calls it 1,000 True Fans: "A creator, such as an artist, musician, photographer, craftsperson, performer, animator, designer, videomaker, or author—in other words, anyone producing works of art—needs to acquire only 1,000 True Fans to make a living."

With one thousand true fans—people "who will purchase anything and everything you produce"—you're more or less guaranteed a livable income provided that you continue to produce consistently great work. It's a small empire and one that requires considerable upkeep, but an empire nonetheless.

Iron Maiden is this idea on a massive scale. Their hard-core fans buy essentially everything they've ever made, which has turned the group into a perennial force in the music industry. It's allowed them to endure through fads, technological shifts, and the fact that their music was never mainstream. Since Iron Maiden has a lot more than one thousand fans, they're living the artist's dream *multiplied by one thousand*. There's even a phrase that the fans say that lets other fans know their identity: *Up the Irons!* I was once invited to a small, private dinner (which I was woefully and embarrassingly unqualified to be a guest at), and for some reason it came up that Iron Maiden was my favorite band. Lance Armstrong, also in attendance, overheard and quietly told me that he

---

* I was trying to illegally download a Metallica song but ended up getting "Hallowed Be Thy Name" from Iron Maiden. I was hooked from that point forward. (Remember what I said about free being an effective advertising tool?)

too was an enormous fan, that he'd grown up listening to the band and had seen them in concert a half dozen times. If I'd just randomly said "Up the Irons," he'd have known exactly what I was talking about.

This incredible bond and platform have meant not only that Iron Maiden is financially successful, but that its members are able to direct their own careers, produce work on their own terms, and speak directly to an audience without undue interference from outsiders or intermediaries. Heavy metal could be made illegal and it probably wouldn't stop Iron Maiden's career.

The question, then, is: How do we build our own loyal audience? How do we communicate with this fan base, and how do we develop the body of work required to support it over the course of a perennially selling career?

What's a Platform?

Michael Hyatt, former CEO of Thomas Nelson Publishers, writes, "In the old days, you could stand on a small hill or a wooden stage to be heard. That was your platform." In the literal sense, that's a platform. This was the tool and the approach you used so that you and your message could reach people. Today, people think of a "platform" a bit differently. Many see it as how many social media followers you have, or the ratings of a television show. I would argue that this definition is almost equally simplistic.

In my definition, a platform is the combination of the tools, relationships, access, and audience that you have to bear on spreading your creative work—not just once, but over the course of a career. So a platform is your social media and the stage you stand on, but it also includes your friends, your body of work, the community your work exists in, the media outlets and influencers who appreciate what you do, your email list, the trust you've built, your sources of income, and countless other assets. A platform is what you cultivate and grow not just *through* your creative work, but *for* your creative work, whatever it may be.

As I said before, Winston Churchill was a brilliant orator and politician who excelled on exactly the literal kind of platform that Michael Hyatt was talking about. Yet he also had a more expansive and modern platform. Most people are unaware that Churchill made his living as a writer, publishing some *ten million* words in his lifetime across hundreds of publications and published works. In fact, it was his enormous worldwide readership that Churchill cultivated through books, newspaper columns, and radio appearances that allowed him to survive the periods in which he was exiled from public life. (During his infamous exile in the so-called political wilderness between 1931 and 1939, Churchill published 11 volumes and more than 400 articles, and delivered more than 350 speeches.) An ordinary politician would have been powerless when pushed out of office or driven to the fringes by political enemies. Not Churchill. His enormous platform—based on his editorial contacts, his extraordinary gift with words, and his relentless energy—allowed him not only to be relevant but also to guide policy and opinion across the globe both in and out of office.

Stefan Zweig, whose quote about building a loyal audience opened this chapter, was at one point one of the most popular novelists in the world. As an Austrian Jew, he was chased from Europe by the rise of Hitler. He made it to the United States and later to Brazil (where sadly he later committed suicide). But even the vicious persecution and attempts by the National Socialists to burn his books were not wholly successful—his work lives on today, and his last two books are powerful, timeless indictments of chaos and authoritarianism.

The ability to access and draw on our assets—whether they are social media or an email list or a phone call to a loyal ally or simply a popular body of work—is what makes an artist successful over the long term. It's also what allows our work to endure even the most heinous attempts at censorship or oppression. A platform is what gives us the ability to launch our work into the world and keep it going once it has been launched so that it may reach perennial status. So it may survive in a hostile and receptive world alike.

As with everything else in this book, the only person who can set this platform is you. Only you can develop your own army of what Lady Gaga calls her "Little Monsters"—the die-hard fans who hang on her every word.*

Marketing is far easier when you have fans and friends like these to count on. Producing your next project is easier when you have a real, direct relationship with an audience and can learn what they like, want, and need. Creating a perennial seller and word of mouth is possible when you have high-level supporters who are willing to evangelize what you do and bring other people to your work. Enjoying a career that lasts decades—which is what most of us want—is possible only if we've built a sustainable enterprise and income stream that allows us to take risks, invest in ourselves, and ride out difficulties and changes in the market.

All of this is why publishers and investors increasingly ask questions geared toward this topic when they are considering working with a creator or entrepreneur. They want to know: *What's your platform? Who is your audience? What's your long-*

---

* One of the best books on platforms is Jackie Huba's *Monster Loyalty: How Lady Gaga Turns Followers into Fanatics.* Check it out.

term plan? They want to be confident that an author or entrepreneur can actually get his or her idea out into the world—that there are people actually interested in hearing about it. These creators represent much safer bets than brilliant unknowns.

Almost every industry is facing the same reality, which is why you have to subject yourself to that same scrutiny: Do I have the reach to pull this off? Is my platform big enough for me to launch yet? What investments can I make now that will lengthen my career by strengthening my audience and fan base? No matter what you're selling, a platform is an invaluable asset.

Why You Need a Platform

Everyone wants a platform when they need one. People want to have a big list—they just don't want to lay the groundwork for one beforehand. They think a robust platform is their God-given right for being so smart and talented. Or they think that since they've been successful in the past, obviously everyone is going to line up to buy whatever they're doing now. Sorry—not how it works.

You see this a lot in film. Hollywood assumes that because they put somebody famous in a movie, that movie will be a success. But fame and platform are not the same. *Star Wars* has a platform of loyal diehards; your average romantic comedy does not and never will. Arnold Schwarzenegger has a platform, one he has meticulously built over the years, allowing him to conquer Hollywood, government, and now social media. Meanwhile, other famous actors, like Charlie Sheen or Katherine Heigl—as well known as they are—have no ability to do something similar.

Casey Neistat was once an up-and-coming filmmaker destined to be the next go-to indie director. He'd created a successful show for HBO. He'd had a film at Sundance. He'd premiered two movies at Cannes. But he left that behind to distribute his work on YouTube. Why? Because the grind of making stuff and then hustling for funding and negotiating with agents and finally waiting for a distributor to get it to an audience was exhausting. It's hard to be an artist when a middleman gets to decide which pieces of your art make it to viewers.

On YouTube, however, he could release his videos directly to his fans. He could line up subscribers. He could reach people directly on social media and via email. Online, he has a platform—one he owns and operates, no middlemen allowed. And you know what? It works to great effect. For over a year he put up a video every single day to millions of subscribers. His daily vlogs racked up hundreds of thousands of views within *hours* of going live each morning. There's no promotional apparatus here, he doesn't lobby a studio for a marketing budget, there's no vying for a release date against the rest of a distributor's slate. Today he's one of the most influential directors on the planet—even if most people who aren't his fans would have trouble recognizing his name.

This is the highest—and over the long term, most profitable—kind of artistic freedom. Casey isn't hoping that YouTube will help him get noticed by Hollywood. He doesn't need it. As he said, "Platform is not a stepping stone. It is the finish line."

That's a powerful—and powerfully counterintuitive—way to think about your work. And the reason more people don't think in this manner is because they are afraid. They're afraid of carving their own path and finding nothing at the end of it. They're overly concerned with the vanity and status consciousness of fans who are comfortable in the traditional system. They want the validation that comes (supposedly) from being given a deal or signed to a contract by an established institution—whether that's a publisher, a studio, an agency, a gallery, or a Fortune 100. Many of us are afraid, to borrow James Altucher's phrase, *to choose ourselves*.

The great Stoic Marcus Aurelius once admonished himself to be a "boxer, not a fencer." A fencer, he said, has to bend down to pick up his weapon. A boxer's weapon is a part of him—"all he has to do is clench his fist." In developing a platform, we eschew the promotional apparatus that must be rebuilt and picked up anew with each and every launch. Instead, we choose to bind ourselves to an audience, to become one with that audience, and to become one with our weapon.

Build Your List. Build Your List. Build Your List.

If I could give a prospective creative only one piece of advice, it would be this: *Build a list*. Specifically, an *email list*. Why? Imagine that, for reasons entirely outside your control, there was a media and industry blackout of your work. Imagine that, due to some controversy or sudden change in public tastes, you were suddenly *persona non grata*. Imagine if no publisher, no crowdfunding platform, no retailer, no distributors, and no investors would touch what you've made.

In any normal scenario—until very recently, in fact—you'd be screwed. You'd have no way to release your product, no way to get your message out into the world. All would be lost.

But, as I said, Iron Maiden wouldn't be screwed. In fact, the situation I described was very much their reality for a long time. Grunge, indie rock, and rap drove heavy metal out of popular culture for years. It's sadly a very real scenario for a lot of artists—because they aren't on trend, because of political winds, because somebody has screwed something up. Suddenly they're facing cultural irrelevance.

The only way to survive that kind of catastrophe is if you have some way to go directly to your people. What if you could avoid all the middlemen and communicate directly with people who care about only one thing: whether they want what you're selling? Well, then you could continue to do what you do.

That way exists. It's called a mailing* list, and it shouldn't take the threat of being frozen out to get one started. Ideally, an email list is something you build up over the years, comprised of real, hard-core fans who know the real story about you and are never going to abandon you as long as what you make continues to be good. Right now, as of this writing, it's the single most important and effective way to communicate with your potential audience and customers. That list is a lifeline, one that can help you thrive when times are good and survive when times are bad.

Building an email list is a move toward self-sufficiency for any creator. By forming a direct and regular line of communication with your supporters, you avoid ever being disintermediated. That is an incredibly powerful asset. Remember taking stock of all your assets in the marketing section? The things you were putting in your spreadsheet? Your email list should be the first entry on the sheet.

After the comedian Kevin Hart experienced several disappointing failures in a row, his career was at a crossroads. The movies he'd expected to make him a star hadn't hit; his television deal hadn't panned out. So he did what comedians do best—he hit the road. But unlike many successful comedians, he didn't just go to the cities where he could sell the most seats. Instead, he went *everywhere*—

---

* Today that means "email list," for the most part, so that's how I am going to use it.

often deliberately performing in small clubs in cities where he did not have a large fan base. At every show, an assistant would put a business card on each seat at every table that said, "Kevin Hart needs to know who you are," and asked for their email address. After the show, his team would collect the cards and enter the names into a spreadsheet organized by location. For four years he toured the country this way, building an enormous database of loyal fans and drawing more and more people to every subsequent show.

As his name grew, Hart began to take television gigs that he thought would allow him to grow his platform. In 2011, he hosted the MTV Music Awards and snagged, by his count, more than 250,000 Twitter followers in one swoop. Across social media and email, Hart's fan-by-fan ground game—in his words, "years of me building and building and building and reaching out to my fans on the personal level"—built up a platform of more than fifty million people, people he could communicate with at the touch of a button.

This asset is so unusual in Hollywood that it actually became controversial when Hart began to leverage it. Negotiations between the actor's representatives and Sony Pictures Studios that leaked during the infamous Sony hacking scandal showed Hart's ability to command higher paydays from the studio in exchange for his willingness to promote on his platform a movie *they'd already paid him to be in*. This infuriated Sony, who seemed to think it was entitled to what Hart built and controlled. One executive called him a "whore" when Hart's production company explained that access to this audience wasn't free. As Hart later posted, he's not a whore—he's the owner of a platform, and access to that platform is valuable. "I worked very hard to get where I am today," he wrote. "I look at myself as a brand and because of that I will never allow myself to be taken advantage of."

Kevin's platform is an important example because it's based, at its core, on email addresses that he and his team gathered in person and by hand over many years and countless club dates. Yes, he has millions of social media followers now too, but it is the email list that is truly the bread and butter of Kevin Hart, Inc. If his movie career were to suddenly implode, he'd still make a killing on the road—because Kevin Hart knows exactly "who you are" and what city to come perform for you in.

Drew Curtis, who created Fark.com, a popular news aggregator now going into its seventeenth year in business (run out of his home in suburban Kentucky), told me something very similar. "The only way to guarantee longevity online is to retain control of your own engagement channel. Mainstream media is learning the hard way what happens when you outsource audience engagement to search engines or social media. For example, my local newspaper has totally trained me to only find them through Twitter. If Twitter decides to start charging them for access to this engagement channel, they're done."

Eight- and nine-figure social media metrics can be very intoxicating, but we should be wary of overinvesting in social platforms, because they come and go—ask all the folks who had large Myspace followings—and it's entirely outside our control. Their policies can change; they can get acquired or go bankrupt. They can suddenly start charging you money for services that you once expected would be free. When we evaluate which platforms to jump into as we build our audience, our old friend the Lindy effect is a fitting rubric to apply. If something has been around for only a month, extrapolating that it's going to last for *at least another month* isn't exactly encouraging given how busy we are and how important the success of our creation is to our career. Meanwhile, email is approaching its fiftieth birthday. Seriously. *Email is almost fifty years old.*

Craigslist, itself a two-decades-old institution, began as an email list that Craig Newmark used to alert his fellow San Franciscans about apartments and events. As he put it to me, "Email, aside from spam, is what people might want to see, and is delivered into one's mailbox, which is almost always in a convenient window. It's pretty much universal." It's now more or less timeless. It helped him build a billion-dollar company that has survived countless competitors, trends, and changes.

Perhaps in the future email will be replaced as the dominant medium by some magical telepathic communication technology that we cannot yet envision. But in the way that radio has survived the invention of cinema, television, and the Internet, email will likely endure in some way. And for right now, it is your best bet, so use it.

Are there other valuable mechanisms? Of course. Seth Godin says that platforms (and thus lists) are built via "permission assets"—a larger bucket that would include everything from Facebook to Twitter to [insert popular platform of the day]. Basically, anything where people can opt in to hear from you.

It's these lists that determine who we're able to launch to, what kind of influence we can bring to bear on a project, and the amount of attention we can assume as a baseline. Chris Lavergne, the founder of Thought Catalog, once made the distinction for me between "a voice among a billion other voices" and an *authority*." An authority is backed by something—by a list and a platform.

But of course, just as platforms don't spring from the earth magically, lists don't just *happen*. They're made.

How to Build It So That They Will Come

In 2008, I came to the realization that while I would one day like to publish a book, unless things changed, I would have no way of actually telling readers about my book. I decided I would build an email list. But what about? I wasn't important or interesting enough for people to just sign up based on my name alone. So I came up with an idea: What if I gave monthly book recommendations? (The thinking being that one day I might recommended one of my own books to this list.) Once a month for four years I sent this list out, and as a result it grew from ninety original sign-ups to the five thousand people to whom I announced my first book. By the time my next book came out two years later, the list was at more than thirty thousand, and today it's at eighty thousand.

After his successful launch of *Choose Yourself*, James Altucher completely embraced self-publishing and all it entailed. He built a podcast that he distributes directly through his email list. He then created an exclusive, high-ticket newsletter that gives financial advice through email. He created a members-only book club. He wrote several more books, selling many of them directly through his website and thus amassing not only hundreds of thousands of email addresses, but physical mailing lists and payment information for his fans as well. It's now a huge platform that, by his estimation, grosses more than $20 million a year in revenue.

You can build a list about anything. A lot of lists are about the people who made them, naturally. There's no reason to sign up for Iron Maiden's list or to friend them on Facebook unless you like Iron Maiden. People who subscribe to Casey Neistat's YouTube channel are interested in getting only his videos. People who give their address to Bed Bath & Beyond are asking to be mailed coupons and informed about upcoming sales. If you want people to consume your work and to know what you do next, you have to make it possible for them to hear about it as easily and regularly as possible.

I once worked with a wonderful nonfiction author whose previous book is an undeniable classic of its genre. It was the kind of perennial seller that publishers dream of. It sold north of one million copies in an era when most sales still came from bookstores instead of online and when publishers could be partly counted on to handle marketing for the author. Ten years later, he was ready to release his next big project, but he had no way to reach any of his readers. He had no social media presence, no media contacts, no email lists. All those millions of fans—and no way of identifying or contacting them. He did *not* have a platform.

This meant that, like far too many successful artists, he had to start from scratch—selling to everyone instead of first reaching out to the people who had purchased his last book and creating quick traction as a result. That's inexcusable. The people who already like his stuff are just supposed to find out serendipitously that there is another book? In this day and age? Still that happens—far too often.

My friend Noah Kagan, the expert marketing mind behind the company AppSumo, calls this "amnesia marketing." Because you keep forgetting your customers, you have to find them over and over again for each project. There is an impulse that is common to those who are prone to this mistake: paying someone to build your list for you. I urge you to avoid compounding one mistake with another. Building your list is not someone else's job. People will not beg you for the opportunity to join it. You can't buy subscribers. No list is built entirely through advertising. It will take work— sometimes years of work—for it to pay off. But it will be worth it.

The best way to create a list is to provide incredible amounts of value. Here are some strategies to help you do that:

- Give something away for free as an incentive. (Maybe it's a guide, an article, an excerpt from your book, a coupon for a discount, etc.)

- Create a gate. (There used to be a Facebook tool that allowed musicians to give away a free song in exchange for a Facebook like or share—that's a gate. BitTorrent does the same thing with its Bundles—some of the content is free, and if you want the rest of it, you've got to fork over an email address.)
- Use pop-ups. (You're browsing a site and liking what you see and *BOOM* a little window pops up and asks if you want to subscribe. I put such pop-ups at the back of all my books.)
- Do things by hand. (I once saw an author pass around a clipboard and a sign-up sheet at the end of a talk. It was old-school, but it worked. Also, at the back of my books I tell people to email me if they want to sign up, and then I sign them up by hand.)
- Run sweepstakes or contests. (Why do you think the lunch place by your office has a fishbowl for business cards? Those cards have phone numbers and email addresses. They give away a sandwich once a week and get hundreds of subscribers in return.)
- Do a swap. (One person with a list recommends that their readers sign up for yours; you email your fans for theirs.)
- Promise a service. (The last one is the simplest and most important. What does your list do for people? Promise something worth subscribing to and you'll have great success.)

Lists vary in size and quality, but they all have one thing in common—they start at zero. I asked Noah, who has built multiple seven-figure businesses off his email lists, how he'd recommend getting your first email subscribers. To get your first one hundred subscribers, Noah recommends doing this:

1. Put a link in your email signature. How many emails do you send a day?

2. See which social networks allow you to export your followers and send them a note asking them to join.
3. Post online once a week asking your friends/family/coworkers to join your mailing list.
4. Ask one group you are active in to join your newsletter.
5. Create a physical form you can give out at events.

That's a pretty decent start, requiring very little effort.

Make no mistake—this list you are building can become, over time, incredibly valuable. I've seen clients sell literally hundreds of thousands of dollars worth of products in a single day from a single email. I've seen authors sell their critical first hundred or thousand copies of a book. I've seen startups get traction right out of the gate, while their competitors struggled, because they had better access to a base audience for whom they had already created great value.

So start building now. Wherever you are, whatever you're doing.

Your Network Is Your Net Worth*

There is a second kind of "list" that matters just as much as the list I've been describing: your list of contacts, relationships, and influencers. You know that saying "It's not what you know, it's *who* you know"? Well, it's true.

My friend and client Tim Ferriss is probably the greatest and most awe-inspiring example of this. When I met Tim, I was nineteen years old and somebody's assistant. Tim was a successful but mostly unknown entrepreneur putting the finishing touches on a

---

* I actually worked on a book with this title. It's good. You should read it.

book nobody thought would sell (it had been rejected by twenty-five out of twenty-six publishers).

What brought us together was the South by Southwest (SXSW) conference in Austin, Texas. For me, it was the first real conference of my life. Tim, well, he was on what I might now describe as a networking tour. Instead of spending money on advertising or publicity, he was traveling from conference to conference to meet as many influential people as possible, developing relationships, learning, and doing favors. He even spent time with me, a total nobody at the time, because my boss was important. Within a few months, he would have a debut *New York Times* bestseller and unbelievable amounts of media coverage and online attention. Within a few years, that book would be translated into more than forty languages, sell millions of copies, and transform countless lives. And almost all of that success can be attributed to the network he built on that conference tour. (That network wouldn't help just with books; it led to advising and investment deals worth millions of dollars as well.)

Some of Tim's strategies:

Never dismiss anyone—You never know who might help you one day with your work. His rule was to treat everyone like they could put you on the front page of the *New York Times* . . . because someday you might meet that person.

Play the long game—It's not about finding someone who can help you right this second. It's about establishing a relationship that can one day benefit *both* of you.

Focus on "pre-VIPs"—The people who aren't well known but should be and will be. It's not about who has the biggest megaphone. A great example for me was meeting Tim. He hadn't sold millions of books then and didn't have a huge platform. Now he does.

As is true for so many things, the best time to have built your network was yesterday. The *second best time* is right now. The best time to get to know people and develop relationships is *before* you have some favor you want to ask them (this is called being a human being). If you're networking for something that's out in a week, you have no leverage. When being introduced to someone, no one wants the first words out of that new acquaintance's mouth to be, "You know what you can do for me?" All you're doing then is begging and imposing. Don't be that person. Be generous, do favors, help other people with their products. Email reporters who cover things that you're interested in (or at least *read* their work and take genuine interest in it).

Networking is *not* going to networking events and handing out business cards—that's *flyering*. It is instead about forming, developing, and maintaining real relationships. It's about being valuable and being available so that one day the favor might be returned.

Relationships Are a Platform Too

In the 2016 Democratic primary, Hillary Clinton beat Bernie Sanders despite his incredible momentum and inspiring, populist rhetoric. Story after story waxed on about Bernie's stunning rise, his impassioned supporters, and his dark-horse candidacy—and yet Hillary Clinton won. Why? Because she'd locked in something unique to the Democratic primary: superdelegates. These delegates account for some 15 percent of the total convention votes, but they are not tied to the outcome of the various state races. Over her years in public service, Hillary locked in these delegates through relationship building, collaboration, and institutional knowledge.

The primary election ultimately wasn't close—because while Sanders appealed simply to the public, Clinton worked behind the scenes to build trust with the ultimate decision makers.*

In the context of politics, this did not seem fair to many primary voters. Some people felt Sanders had been cheated, even though he did not win a majority of votes, let alone superdelegates. And as if Hillary's putting in the work to build relationships instead of giving rousing speeches was not the *essence* of modern politics (and life, for that matter).

It's a common, misguided attitude in creative circles too. The comedian Marc Maron perfectly encapsulates how we feel when we see a peer or competitor snag some big opportunity or score a big break. In such moments of jealousy and envy, we say, "How did *you* get *that*?" The emphasis there on "you" is important, as in, "It should have been me," and the "that," as in, "You don't deserve something so great." We're mad that others were more successful than us, that somehow everything seemed to break their way, perhaps bitter that people opened doors for them and not for us.

This is not only a miserable way to live, but it also misses the point. No one is entitled to relationships only because their work is genius. Relationships have to be earned, and maintained. If your goal is to become a grand master of important relationships, make sure you're playing chess and not checkers. You better make sure that you don't overemphasize giving rousing speeches to your troops at the cost of shoring up relationships with critical allies. Doing this work is not only important marketing, it's essential to establishing a viable and valuable platform.

---

* Clinton's subsequent loss in the general election illustrates another point: All the influencers in the world are meaningless if you can't also motivate the masses and drive them to take action.

Developing the right relationships with the right people is the long game. This is how legacies are made and preserved. The new album that is suddenly everywhere and being talked about by everyone? This doesn't just happen—it's the result of assiduously courting the right influencers, and maybe having brought on a producer who already had those relationships. The entrepreneur who gets another shot after a failure? That's the result of having built up trust with investors, having communicated and shown why he's worth a second chance. The brilliant biography with all sorts of new revelations? That's because the author spent years getting to know the family, becoming friends with the librarian who manages the archive, with proving herself as being someone that people can open up to. In all these cases, the creator is putting in work that will ultimately give the creation a better platform to launch from.

As I said earlier, everyone wants an email list but few want to put in the effort to make one. I've also found that people have the same attitude about *other* people's lists. They want to call in favors or have friends or fellow creators market their products to their fans for them, but few stop to ask: Why should someone do me this huge favor? The only proper answer to that question is: Because I've done them favors in the past—because I've built up karmic debt.

If you see your career and your relationships as investments— if you give and help and build long before you ever need anything, if you continue doing great work over the long term—you'll find that sometimes you won't even need to ask for support. Your friends and supporters will come to you. They'll offer.

Yet too many creators think that this will just happen. Or others are so shortsighted they think they can acquire this valuable asset on a pay-per-play basis—as if purchased influence would ever really be that influential. Think about it this way: You can pay for influence the way you can pay for sex, but from what I understand neither is quite the same as when you get it the old-fashioned way. Just as earned media is always better than paid media, cultivating real influence and relationships is far better than paying for eyeballs and fake friends.

The Most Important Relationship

While relationships with the "in crowd" matter and they help create an enduring career, nothing you build will last very long without the most important relationship of all: the one you have with your fans. Imagine if at some point in their career Iron Maiden decided to see their fans as dollar signs instead of human beings. How quickly would all those years of work have been undone? For decades, the band has made serving and satisfying their fans their number one priority. One music writer described their style of music and fan interaction as "populist without being pandering." *That* is what has allowed them to survive changing trends, a blacklist from mainstream radio, different lead singers, and every other storm the fates have sent their way.

It can't be, as Lady Gaga warned, "Thanks for buying my record, fuck you." Your relationship with your fans must be more than transactional. It must be deeper. It should be for *life*. As she explained, she wants to tell her fans, "Thank you for buying my record—and I will live and die and breathe my art to protect your dreams because you protect mine." There's another line from one of the founding members of the band Twisted Sister, now in its fourth decade as a group. At a certain point in his career, Jay Jay French, the band's guitarist, said he realized that he wasn't in the music business—*he was in the Twisted Sister business*. Meaning, the only people who matter to him are Twisted Sister fans.

Barbara Hendricks, founder of a prestigious book PR firm (having represented authors like Jack Welch and Clayton Christensen), put it like this: "Authors who want long-term success should adopt this mantra: Participate. Participate. Participate." But forget authors. *People* who want long-term success must participate—and do so authentically and honestly.

The reason successes like Lady Gaga's or Twisted Sister's are rare—in music or in business—is that very few people follow that logic and participate in a meaningful way. Mostly we see the opposite behavior. *Forbes*, for example, is a hundred-year-old media brand. After spending a century earning a solid reputation for financial journalism, the outlet embraced the trend of opening its site up to contributors (essentially, *anyone*). *Time* did the same thing, and so did many other prestigious outlets. It might seem as if opening their platforms up to more and more writers is a form of participation, but it is participation in a relationship with the wrong group. For a short time, of course, these outlets were able to arbitrage the difference between perception (exclusive, prestigious journalism) and reality (unedited amateur contributors). Eventually, though, the exploitation inherent in their strategic choice took a toll on the brand, primarily because it *took a toll on the trust between the publications and their readers*—the group with whom they *should* have been participating in a relationship.

When we said the Lindy effect means that the things that last would continue to last, the exception to that rule is when owners undermine what made them great in the first place. Perennial sales are not guaranteed. Hard-won reputations can be undone. Fans, once chewed up and spit out, do not come back. Conversely, the more intimate and personal the connection between creator, work, and fan, the more the relationship can endure. You do not want to

be on the wrong side of the ledger when it comes to your relationships and karmic debt. You never want to owe.

Think of a creator you've been a fan of for years. How have
they managed to keep your attention? It isn't just making something great once and riding that success into the sunset—it's how
great the band is in concert, it's the thirtieth-anniversary special,
it's the way the creator gives such great interviews, it's the emails
you've received or their presence on social media (you know, the
posts where it feels like they're actually writing to you and not
everyone else). Most of all, it's that, after this was done over and
over again for a group of people in the same field, a community
began to emerge—and now you are a part of that community.

It's on you to bring that kind of thoughtfulness and care to
your own work and the platform you're building to sell it on.

Settle In for the Long Haul

In 1962, the scientist Thomas Kuhn wrote a short book titled *The
Structure of Scientific Revolutions*. His thesis was controversial—
that scientific change doesn't follow a line of steady linear progress. Essentially, he argued that scientists in every era have
assumptions and beliefs that guide their work. Change happens as
these beliefs begin to break down and bold new theories that
change the way everything is seen are proposed in their place. This
is what he calls a "paradigm shift."

Ironically, the trajectory of his book is a pretty good example
of the old gradual way—it was hardly a paradigm shift at publication. It sold only 919 copies its first year. But fifty years later, it has
sold more than a *million* copies worldwide.

I think most people hope what they're doing will be suddenly
received as a bold work of staggering genius that sells a million

copies *immediately*. Obviously, this is the preferred path to success. Who wants to wait a half century? What good is a successful product after you're old and gray? Or dead, if you're among the impressionist painters who died penniless but whose work today hangs in the world's finest museums?

Most people want instant gratification, debut bestseller status, a launch that puts them in the pantheon right away. Let's call that strategy what it is: a wild sprint. The reality is that the race to creative success today is really a marathon. Barbara Hendricks explains to authors how misguided their timelines often are: "I urge authors to consider how long it took them to write their books and see them published and to devote at least that much time to pushing them."

That seems doable, right? You can work at supporting your art at least as long as you worked in the creation phase of it. At the very minimum, a fifty-fifty split is way more reasonable than the four-to-one ratio my entrepreneur friend talked about at the very start of the book. Regardless, don't you think you owe it to your work to give it an honest chance to find success before you write yourself off? Your movie took years to develop, but you're going to let the distributor just pull it after opening weekend without fighting to give your audience another chance to see it? C'mon.

Nor are we really asking you to do anything that crazy. Remember, the music industry defines a catalog album as starting at eighteen months. You can stay committed for that long, right? You can give your work the same amount of time to get its legs as you would a toddler, right?

As Seth Godin has written:

> The launch is the launch. What happens after the launch, though, isn't the result of momentum. It's the result of a dif-

ferent kind of showing up, of word of mouth, of the book (or whatever tool you're using to cause change) being part of something else, something bigger.

It's hard to put it better than Alexandre Dumas does in an exchange in *The Count of Monte Cristo*. In it, the pretentious Danglars is showing off his expensive art collection, specifically his paintings from the "old masters." "I do not like the modern school," he says, expressing his disdain for the popular work of the day (which, as it happens, was early-nineteenth-century Parisian art). To which the sarcastic Monte Cristo replies, "You are quite right, Monsieur. On the whole, they have one great shortcoming, which is that they have not yet had the time to become old masters."

It's not that reputation is some long, hard slog. It's just that, like your platform, it requires time, effort, and dedication to build. And time—again, lots of time. Audiences often need to hear about things multiple times and be exposed to them from multiple angles before they're willing to give something a chance. The same logic applies to you as a creator, to giving you a chance. The momentum necessary to create that kind of lift takes time to build. You have to give yourself the runway to get airborne. To cut the engines halfway through? That's the best way to ensure you never leave the ground.

It's worth remembering that Hollywood record books are littered with "holiday blockbusters" that opened huge on Christmas Day only to be surpassed a few short years later (some even sooner) by perennial favorites like *Elf* and *A Christmas Story*—movies watched only one month a year that keep chugging along like the proverbial tortoise racing the hare.*

* This is not a unique phenomenon. *Star Wars* was beaten in its opening weekend by *Smokey and the Bandit*—$2.7 million to $2.5 million.

Plenty of projects get off to slow starts through no fault of their own. Hemingway's *A Farewell to Arms* was released on the day the markets crashed in 1929. Robert Greene's *The Art of Seduction* came out shortly after the events of September 11, 2001. Neil Strauss's *The Game* was scheduled for release the week after Hurricane Katrina hit. All the expected press for these authors, along with their precious launch windows, were obliterated. It's not as if these wildly successful authors lacked an audience, mind you. It was just that their audience had bigger things on their minds in that particular moment. That's life. But you have persevere. If a few press hits and a single day of sales were all the heart they had in their respective launches, they would have been finished.

A launch is important, but we must bear in mind what Kafka's publisher wrote to his author after poor sales: "You and we know that it is generally just the best and most valuable things that do not find their echo immediately." In other words, it is far better to measure your campaign *over a period of years, not months.*

One of the comedians my company has worked with, Ralphie May, does something like three hundred shows a year. As he explained, "There's no such thing as a great stand-up who was born great. Every one of them sucked when they started and worked their asses off to get great. I've been doing stand-up for twenty-five years and I do three hundred shows a year. That's how I got great." It's also how he got big! No comedian is born popular or born with an audience—not a big one anyway. They earn it. On the road, on TV, in movies, and anywhere else they can be funny and get exposure.

Ian Fleming once wrote to his publisher, "I bet your other authors don't work as hard for you as I do." He was right. Most think they're too good for it, or they are too sensitive to push hard enough. I remember early on I asked my agent Stephen Hanselman what separated his bestselling clients from his smaller ones. He said, "Ryan, success almost always requires an unstoppable author." Throughout my career, I've seen this played out not just in books but in all products.

Marketing Can't Stop. The Work Can't Stop. The Hustle Can't Stop. It Must Go On and On.

Once you have started to see the slow accumulation of success for a work over the long haul, you can't quit on a project. There are many things you can do to continue to update and expand your work. Think of all the twentieth-anniversary editions out there, the "revised and expanded" updates to keep a book or guide current, the "newly remastered" albums and the collector's versions of classic products. Part of the reason that the first generation of rock and roll bands have done so well financially over the years has been their ability to take advantage of technological innovations. The Eagles sold records, eight-tracks, cassettes, CDs, MP3s, Spotify spins, and now, because irony is dead, they're selling vinyl records again. There's a reason that book publishers put exciting new covers on classic books every few years ("old book, new look") and assign new translators every few decades. The first book Harper-Collins ever published was actually a translation of the ancient Stoics. Today their imprints are *still* publishing various versions of those texts. The first Penguin Classics in 1964 was a translation of *The Odyssey*, which almost immediately sold more than 3 million copies. Penguin Classics is now an entire franchise, celebrating its fiftieth anniversary. The underlying work stays the same, but they are breathing new life into it by staying on top of trends. They aren't letting their offering become old or tired.

Wouldn't Craigslist have been well served to try to add at least *some* new features over the years? Why was there still no "edit" button on Twitter nearly ten years into the service's history? Not that anyone should have sacrificed their classic design, but small continual improvements make a big difference. Basecamp certainly hasn't lost anything rebuilding its core features every four years—it's helped it last longer. The Pantry in Downtown LA might not accept credit cards, but they did put an ATM at the front to make paying easier.

No one can guarantee that your project will be a success, but it can be safely said that if you quit on it before your audience does, it's guaranteed to fail. If you let it rot or ossify, you will shorten its life. If you take your customers for granted, they will eventually find somewhere else to go. Give yourself some time and some runway, then. You're going to want it.

Build a Body of Work

That this book is split into two parts—the first half about creation and the second half about marketing—might lead you to believe that the proper ratio of your overall effort is fifty-fifty. That would be a mistake. Because even when we have our "marketing hat" on, we're still thinking of ways to produce and to make. *Making is also marketing.*

Let me explain. An author kills himself to write a book, throws everything he has into marketing it, and then, in a conversation with another, much more successful author, asks: "What else should I do? How can I make sure my book keeps selling?" It is at this juncture—reached by many an author over the years—that this well-meaning creator is given one of the most frustrating pieces of advice ever designed: The best marketing you can do for your book is to *start writing the next one.*

It is frustrating because it is depressingly, frustratingly true. More great work is the best way to market yourself.

Likewise, the best thing an actor can do—whether it's after an enormous blockbuster or an enormous bomb—is to find her next role, unless she wants to be defined by the previous role.* Same goes for the entrepreneur—whether her company has just sold or just failed, the best thing she can do for her career? Start the next company.

Would *The Godfather* be as good just by itself? It is the trilogy that makes it so iconic and culture-defining. Would *The Iliad* be as popular without *The Odyssey*, or vice versa? Would *The Hobbit* be as popular without *The Lord of the Rings*? Would anyone care about Shakespeare's sonnets without the plays? Or the comedies without the tragedies? Or *Henry IV, Part 1* without *Henry IV, Part 2*?

In fact, creating more work is one of the most effective marketing techniques of all. Robert Greene saw his sales really begin to grow after his *third* book. This was enough for it to be seen as a series. The three books provided enough of a combined sales record for retailers to run promotions around them. Nassim Taleb's four bestselling books—*Fooled by Randomness*, *The Black Swan*, *The Bed of Procrustes*, and *Antifragile*—are now known and marketed collectively as the *Incerto*: "four nonoverlapping volumes that can be accessed in any order." But remember, this was built by publishing one book after another. With my own writing, I got more support from the publisher's sales team after my fourth book than I did for my first, second, or third. It took

---

* In fact, there is an interesting argument put forth by economists like Arthur De Vany that the whole concept of a movie star is created not by roles played but by the advertising campaigns for a film. Each release is a publicity opportunity that increases the fame of the actor, regardless of how the movie ends up faring.

time to win their interest—in a way, to prove that I had what it took. *Moby-Dick* wasn't Herman Melville's first book, and it wasn't his last either. And while *Moby-Dick* might not have experienced much commercial success at the outset, it's unlikely that it would have ever eventually become the classic it became had Melville been a nobody or quit writing in underappreciated disgust.

The idea that good work compounds itself is not just anecdotal. A study done by economists Alan Sorensen and Ken Hendricks explored this phenomenon in music. It turns out that with each new album, the sales of a band's previous album will increase. As the researchers wrote, "Various patterns in the data suggest the source of the spillover is information: a new release causes some uninformed consumers to discover the artist and purchase the artist's past albums." In fact, sales of non-debut albums increase by an average of 25 percent because of this additional discovery and exposure.

Nor does this phenomenon necessarily limit itself to art. Apple didn't make the iPod or iPhone and then stop. It has made new and improved versions of those products almost on a yearly basis for more than a decade now. Each time, the media and customer anticipation only grows bigger. Each of the company's new products is integrated with its other products, hooking users deeper into the Apple universe.

This was an explicit part of Steve Jobs's business strategy as well as his personal strategy. As he said, "If you do something and it turns out pretty good, then you should go do something else wonderful, not dwell on it for too long. Just figure out what's next." Think about Woody Allen—he does a movie nearly every year, and has for decades. He explained that he goes for "quantity" as a way to get to quality. "If you make a lot of films," he said, "occasionally a great one comes out. Films never come out in the end how you expect them to at the start."

Which is why you have to stay at it. Jerry Seinfeld still performs multiple shows a week—and is just as rigorous about his creative process now as he was when the idea of *Seinfeld* was just a joke between him and Larry David. In 2012, the *New York Times* profiled a video in which Seinfeld deconstructs his joke-creating process; the joke the piece focuses on took two years to finish. He's also talked about another joke—a simple line about how a tuxedo is a piece of clothing designed for when you need to fool a small group of people for a short period of time—that took *seven years* to perfect. This is, of course, a comedian who makes millions of dollars off residuals, is a household name, and has absolutely no need to keep performing in dingy clubs and spending an eternity perfecting his jokes. And even those jokes that took years to craft are not secure, since Seinfeld culls about 10 percent of his material from his act each year, saying he fires it the way Jack Welch used to do with underperformers. This means that his act is constantly refreshed and never dated—it also means people can see him on tour every couple of years and know they're not getting the exact same show as last time.

Conversely, the comedian Louis C.K. tosses out his entire one-hour act every single year. He perfects it, polishes it, records it as a special, and then moves on to the next one. It's why he's not only gotten better each year, but also given new fans something to sink their teeth into from the past. Both Louis C.K. and Seinfeld are creating bodies of work that allow them to reach new fans as well as to continue to serve and bring joy to their existing audiences.

"You go from project to project with your heart in your mouth," John McPhee has said. Abandoning proven material or comfortable stomping grounds to start from scratch is a scary prospect because, as McPhee reminds us, "Your last piece will never write your next one for you." Each time you do this, it not only increases your mastery in your chosen craft, but as a result it also increases your odds of creating something brilliant and lasting. The key is that you must do it—you must create, create, create.

I'm not saying that you should just go around wildly saying yes to every opportunity and hoping that one of them sticks. That's the misguided attitude of most publishers, studios, and labels. If they were a little more discerning and focused on the long term instead of chasing every soon-to-be-forgotten trend, they wouldn't have to accept such high failure rates (most books don't earn out their advances, most bands don't hit it big, most movies fail). We're open to opportunities when they present themselves, of course, but we're still carefully selecting our shots—swinging only at the pitches that are over the plate and in our wheelhouse. Which is to say, we are engaging only with the ideas that have the opportunity to be perennial because we are the ones best suited to execute them.

As I see it, not everyone who publishes a book is *an author*. He or she is just someone who *has published* a book. The best way to become an *author* is to write more books, just as a true *entrepreneur* starts more than one business. The best way to become a true comedian, filmmaker, designer, or entrepreneur is to never stop, to keep going. Obviously there are exceptions to this—there are plenty of brilliant creators who have made only one thing. They are still entrepreneurs just as Harper Lee is clearly an author. But wouldn't the world be a better place if Ralph Ellison had written another book? Hopefully Mark Zuckerberg will start another company someday. Why should anyone's first product or project be the end of it?

It's not enough to make one great work. You should try to make a lot of it. Very few of us can afford to abandon our gift after our first attempt, convinced that our legacy is secured.* Nor should we. We should prove to the world and to ourselves that we can do it again . . . and again.

Reach Out to New Fans

One of the things all creatives must do during their downtime is explore new ways of reaching new fans. It doesn't matter how popular your product or your act is, or how long you've been doing it. To all the people who haven't heard about it—which is almost always *the majority of the population*—it's still new.

In this way, marketing is an ongoing process. The responsibility of finding and reaching new fans is an endless task. It's why successful people often collaborate with one another—in order to swap audiences.

Aerosmith does a song with Run-DMC. Ray Charles records *Genius Loves Company*—his bestselling and most award-winning album—with a famous collaborator on every track. Tony Bennett does a joint album with Lady Gaga. Kanye West and Adidas make exclusive sneakers. Uber introduces Spotify inside its app. Robert Greene writes a book with 50 Cent. Floyd Mayweather appears on *Dancing with the Stars*.

---

* Earlier, I mentioned Alexandre Dumas's joke about giving the new school time to become old and classic. He wasn't content to simply wait either. Between 1841 and 1850 alone, he wrote forty-one novels, twenty-three plays, and six travel books. It was enough work to create a few timeless classics.

What was the net result of these little creative experiments? New fans for both creators.

This is something that many niche acts come to terms with. If you're known as a "Latino comedian," your career options are limited—there are only certain venues, certain shows, certain crowds available to you. To cross over, the comedian has to consciously expand her audience and steadily recruit fans from other groups and communities. Maybe that means playing smaller clubs in different cities, or tweaking some sets to be more general and inclusive, or taking a pay cut to be in a movie with universal appeal in order to get in front of a wider audience.

Columnists think about this a lot too; so do television hosts. Every day you go out and perform for your audience. But some days you might put something out expressly designed to appeal to people who are not your audience. Writing a column that goes viral, doing a serious show if you're normally funny, having an atypical guest on—it can be anything. The key is to know that there is a difference between something that services your audience and something that expands it. Call it the "One for Them, One for Me" strategy. In a good career, there's room for both.

As Goethe's maxim goes, "The greatest respect an author can have for his public is never to produce what is expected but what he himself considers right and useful for whatever stage of intellectual development has been reached by himself and others." This is true for *any* type of creative person. After all, repeating yourself is rarely the recipe for winning over new fans. Jerry Seinfeld and Louis C.K. figured this out early on, which is partly why they have been so consistently successful for so long.

That means: Don't be afraid to try crazy things. Don't let your brand tie you down to the point where you don't explore or experiment. It is precisely these little endeavors that might illuminate a new direction for your career. They might expose you to a new community or group who will eat up your other work. Keep yourself from getting stale. Choose never to become so settled into a rut or routine or type that you are constrained by it.

Some people are not your fans and never will be. But there is still something to be done there: Colonel Parker, the infamous manager of Elvis Presley, came up with the idea to sell "I Hate Elvis" memorabilia so that Elvis could profit from his haters too. Everyone should know who their detractors are and rile them up every once in a while just for fun.

Build an Empire

A few years ago I worked on a book project with two very successful hip-hop moguls. They wanted to teach aspiring entrepreneurs the difference between starting a business and *creating an empire*. A lot of people do the former; far fewer manage to pull off the latter.

The book ended up stalling out due to busy schedules, which made me sad because I personally learned a ton just from hearing their way of thinking. That notion of *empire*—expanding into adjacent industries, starting companies, building new brands, grooming protégés, growing bigger and stronger—seems to be a much more natural part of hip-hop than other creative fields. The path from hustler to artist to mogul is a well-trod one, from P. Diddy to Birdman to Jay Z. Maybe rappers are just more ambitious than other artists. In any case, I love their approach. They see business as art too. They don't just want to make music; they want to make music that lets them take over the world.

There's another reality of creative businesses that we need to consider: Most of the real money isn't in the royalties or the sales.

For authors, the real money comes from speaking, teaching, or consulting. Silicon Valley entrepreneurs might do well by their business, but they might do even better investing in their friends' companies. For musicians, the money isn't in records; it's in touring, T-shirts, and eventually endorsements and other products. Michael Jackson, who certainly did well as an artist, arguably did better as an investor *in other artists.* His empire of copyrights and music libraries, which he bought up over the course of his career, generates hundreds of millions of dollars in revenue to this day. Most famously, he bought the rights to the Beatles catalog—partly because he believed it was worth more than the Beatles did (a decision they came to regret).

But for a lot of artists, a fixation on the purity of their craft both prevents them from capitalizing on these channels and actually holds them back from exposing their work to more people. In the 1980s, artists and critics used to sneer at bands like Iron Maiden, Metallica, and AC/DC who "sold more T-shirts than albums." This was somehow supposed to be a slur because, coming from people who love music, if you're not a big seller, you must suck.

Well, the joke was on them. Not only are the margins a lot better on shirts than they are on albums, but *shirts are free advertising for the band.* There are people walking around in vintage Iron Maiden and AC/DC shirts they've had for twenty years. Other people see those shirts and check the music out—then go to concerts and buy their own shirts. It's that expanded empire of products that has helped these bands stay relevant even in the decades since radio stopped playing their stuff. This entrepreneurial mindset—in the case of bands, a willingness to explore potential business opportunities outside of just writing and selling music—is something that every creative needs to consider. Especially in a world where technological innovation has disrupted the markets for selling things like music, books, or products.

Steven Johnson recently produced an extensive study for the *New York Times* on the boom of creative industries. Instead of the rise of the Internet destroying the market for creative work—as many predicted—he found it's had the opposite effect. For some artists anyway—not all. Why? As Johnson observed, "[Our] new environment may well select for artists who are particularly adept at inventing new career paths rather than single-mindedly focusing on their craft." In other words, it's favoring people who can move horizontally and integrate vertically, who can create innovative empires, not just produce work.

Some questions to ask yourself:

What are new areas that my expertise or audience would be valuable in? (Think of celebrities investing in companies or starting their own.)

Is it possible to cut out the middleman like a label or a VC and invest in myself? (Like when musicians buy back their masters or authors get their rights reverted. Jay Z has a famous line that says if you don't own your masters, you're a slave—which is partly true.)

Can I help other artists or creatives achieve what I have achieved? (Be a consultant, coach, or publisher/label head/producer.)

What are other people in my field afraid to do? What do they look down on? (These are almost always great opportunities.)

What can I do to make sure that I am not dependent on a single income stream? (You never know what can happen.)

If I took a break from creating, what would I do instead? (Maybe there is some long-lost passion to rekindle.)

What are parts of the experience or community surrounding my work that I can improve or grow? (Live events, conferences, memberships, personalized products, etc.)

Every industry has its own opportunities. Academics consult. Literary authors teach at universities. Hemingway and Steinbeck both appeared in advertisements; Hemingway even wrote them. Michael Lewis and Malcolm Gladwell both contributed to a campaign for Chipotle. Gladwell is a regular on the speaking circuit. Bruce Dickinson, the lead singer of Iron Maiden, has a radio show, has written a young adult novel, has led a successful solo career, nearly made the British Olympic fencing team, is a professional pilot, and has founded his own aviation company with revenues of $6 million per year. Who knows—maybe Woody Allen has made a couple extra bucks playing his clarinet.

One musician I've worked with, Nick van Hofwegen, known to his fans as Young & Sick, has built a second career for himself as a designer and artist, which connects nicely to his music. While music releases may come only every few months, Van Hofwegen consistently puts out artwork to bring in more fans. His daily Instagram posts are met with thousands of likes and people tagging their friends in the comments to check out his most recent creation. He has created iconic album covers for multiplatinum musicians, including Maroon 5, Foster the People, Robin Thicke, Skrillex, and others. His art for Foster the People was adapted into the biggest mural on the West Coast, at 150 feet by 130 feet, taking up the entire side of a building in downtown Los Angeles.

At the BUKU Festival in New Orleans, the fifteen thousand

daily attendees see Young & Sick creations in every corner of the event, from the stage banners to the festival brochure. Outside of doing all the branding for BUKU, Van Hofwegen has created merchandise for massive festivals like Austin City Limits, which is attended by more than 170,000 people each year. His characters have also found their way into the mainstream as well. They've shown up on Pringles cans, Coors Light advertisements, and even a pair of underwear for the site MeUndies.com, which sold tens of thousands of pairs in their initial run.

As you can imagine, the relationships Van Hofwegen's built working for bigger and more famous musicians as well as while designing materials for big music festivals has also presented musical opportunities. In fact, it would be difficult to separate the two—the artistic ventures support and spread the music, while the music supports and accompanies the art. Most important, the great fear that this will somehow be a distraction or will take away from his production has not come to pass.

Nor is it the case for the most successful multidisciplinary creators.

Google still makes most of its money from search, but it has known for some time that it couldn't *just* be a search engine company, so it has expanded and built addictive products. Now I'm using one such product to write this (Google Docs, which was built by acquiring the company Writely), another to email my editor (Gmail, built internally), and another to waste time with (YouTube, also an acquisition).

Ian Fleming knew that the only way he'd make "proper money" as a writer was to get his books turned into films. So he worked tirelessly to create those opportunities. Rappers after *real* money have to do the same thing. How long can they expect to stay at the top of the charts? (Which charts are becoming increasingly irrelevant anyway.) With this in mind, they pursue other businesses and fund those ventures with their royalties. When you make your money on fashion lines or in movies or club appearances or endorsements or creating your own label—Jay Z, for example, has made far more this way than he has from album sales—then the music becomes a branding device. It becomes a way to reach people. It becomes a loss leader.

That's not a bad thing. It's not "corporatization." If anything, Jay's music has gotten better over the years because he can invest more in it—from music videos to production quality to novel release strategies. Since it all funds a larger empire, he doesn't have to sing for his supper. He sings because he wants to.

In my own career, I was able to take a much lower advance for my second book—a book about Roman philosophy—because the company I had founded around my first marketing book was making enough to support me through the writing process. My empire didn't corrupt my art; it funded it. In fact, that book ended up far outselling the previous one.

What I mean to say is that sometimes the best way to monetize your work—and we do have to make money to live—is not from the work itself, at least not in the short term. We know that perennial sellers can be immensely profitable over time, but they need room to grow, and what better place to grow them than in the fertile ground of your own budding empire?

One Last Thing

Very few people get into creative fields to do *one* thing. Most of us have more than one book in us, more than one film, and even if we have only one company in us, we'll probably want it to have more than one product over its lifetime.

Diversity and productivity are critical parts of that type of longevity. But they require the ability to experiment, to try new things, and to support a body of work, which in turn requires the development of independence and infrastructure. Short of a trust fund or a patient, deep-pocketed patron, there is only one way to do that.

A platform.

To do our work without a platform is to be at the mercy of other people's permission. Someone else must fund us, someone else must give us the green light, someone else must choose to let us make our work. To a creative person, that is death. Having an audience that we own? That we're bound together with like hand and fist? That is life. Yet as I've said before: This does not just happen. It must be built.

So don't wait. Build your platform now. Build it before your first great perennial seller comes out, so that you have a better chance of actually turning it into one. Build it now so that you might create *multiple* works like that. Build it so you can have a career—so you can be more than just a guy or gal with a book or movie or app. Because you're more than that. You're an entrepreneur, an author, a filmmaker, a journalist. You're a mogul.

Don't just make it. Make it happen.

CONCLUSION

What's Luck Got to Do with It?

❧❀❧

There are many things within creators' control: What they decide to work on and the attitude they bring to their work. Their ability to refine their creation and position that work properly. The energy and resources they throw at marketing. The platform they build and the audience they cultivate before and after they've made something.

These are critical factors. No author, no entrepreneur, no maker of any kind is likely to succeed without them. But there is one other important ingredient to success that is not in our control, and it's one we haven't talked about yet in this book: *luck*.

It would be dishonest to talk about creating a classic, perennial seller and pretend that luck has nothing to do with it. Because luck matters a lot. John Fante, the author whose story I've told throughout these pages, saw his career nearly ruined by *bad* luck and then remade decades later in a stroke of amazingly *good* luck.

Luck is polarizing. The successful like to pretend it does not exist. The unsuccessful or the jaded pretend that it is everything. Both explanations are wrong. No matter what we have heard from our parents and internalized as part of the American Dream, hard work does not trump all. At the very, very top, the world is not a simple meritocracy, and it never has been. As Nassim Taleb puts it, "Hard work will get you a professorship or a BMW. You need both work and luck for a Booker, a Nobel or a private jet."

Just ask Bruce Springsteen. *Born to Run*—and by extension, Springsteen's career—has a story defined by pure and unadulterated luck. Two totally unplanned but incredibly fortuitous events occurred that helped make the album—now celebrating its fortieth anniversary and some six million copies sold—the monster success that it eventually became.

The first lucky break happened when, mistakenly assuming that the album was nearly done, Springsteen and the label released "Born to Run" as the lead radio single. But the record was delayed and the single got some six months of unexpected radio play before the album came out. This soft launch was totally accidental—in fact, contrary to their plans—but the fluke created much-needed buzz and runway for the album itself.

Second, Springsteen had struggled with a relatively unsupportive label up until that point. In a moment of frustration, he complained about their contentious relationship in an interview with a college newspaper reporter. It just so happened that the label's new president had a son who attended that very college. The kid read the article and passed it to his father, who reached out to bury the hatchet with Bruce. Their improved relationship meant he was finally able to launch a major record with the true force of a supportive label behind him.

In other words, Bruce had made a masterpiece. He had spent the extra time polishing and positioning it (in fact, that was why its release was delayed). He had begun to build a platform for himself. Yet if the single hadn't been released prematurely and if some kid hadn't read an article in his school paper, things might have turned out very differently.

There's another thing about this Bruce Springsteen anecdote that bears mentioning. *Born to Run* was his *third* album. He'd signed his major label deal several years prior, but he was still struggling to find success. Yet he stayed at it. In that sense, getting lucky wasn't an accident. It's that old saying: The more you do, the harder you work, the luckier you seem to get.

Still, that's pretty terrifying, isn't it? That an artist can do everything right and it still might not work out? Or that it might still involve years of demoralizing struggle against massive odds? And the X factor in all of it is . . . *luck?!?*

What Happens If We Don't Get Lucky?

As I was finishing an early draft of this book, someone recommended that I watch a documentary about MxPx, a punk band I'd listened to a lot as a kid. The documentary opens with the band celebrating its twenty-second year as a group. They'd released sixteen albums, twenty singles, and three films, sold more than 2.5 million records, and toured hundreds of thousands of miles on every continent but Antarctica. I remember watching the Super Bowl on TV in high school and seeing them in a commercial. That's as big as it gets, right?

I'd always held MxPx up as a model for one kind of artist's career. Their success meant that it was possible to *make it* without selling out or courting fame. In many ways, I based my own career around this idea. I wanted to be successful without being *massive*.

And yet—and this nearly made me choke up—the documentary begins with the band as they are more or less deciding to break up. The band was having financial problems. They were tired. Two of the three members had decided to stop touring and take full-time jobs in the shipyards near where they grew up, just as their fathers had done a generation before. It was like the reverse of a Springsteen song. Instead of the dream taking them out of their small industrial town, it showed them all that was possible in the world and then cruelly dropped them back off there in their mid-thirties?

It can't end like this, I thought as I watched it. The very thing that had inspired me to pursue my own career was starting to feel like a lie. Do nice guys really come in last? Small-town kids chase their dream, hit it big, and never sell out, but at the end of the day have to get regular nine-to-five jobs like the rest of us? I was depressed for weeks after. I felt guilty, as if I'd messed up as a fan. *Did I not support them enough? Was it because people just pirate music these days? Did the label screw them?* I wanted someone to blame. I wanted some explanation that this was an anomaly and that it wasn't fair.

As a creator myself, I was worried too, about my career and my own ability to support myself as a writer. Was it possible to accomplish so much and still have to struggle? *Was this how it was going to be for me too?*

As I struggled with these questions, it occurred to me that I could take advantage of one of the privileges of being a writer and just ask the band directly. I reached out to them, under the vague pretense of interviewing them for this marketing book, but the reality was I just needed to know: Was I wrong about perennial sellers? Had I been naive? Was there something I was missing about the arc of their career? Did they screw up somehow? Could I some-day find myself in the same spot in my own career?

I finally reached Mike Herrera, the band's founder, lead singer, and songwriter, after he'd returned from a tour in Europe. Talking to this generous, friendly, and patient man, I realized I was being ridiculous and silly.* Not only because, as it turns out, the band kept going and began recording together again shortly after the documentary came out. (They're just spending less time on the road—a privilege they have certainly earned—and the jobs two of them had gotten doing work on nuclear submarines paid very well.) But secondly, and surprisingly, the band members—despite every right to be—had no bitterness about their journey through the music business.

"It's hard for people to understand that a band that toured constantly and seemingly was on top of the world had to get real jobs. It's like—wow, that's reality," he told me. "But at the same time, reality isn't that bad. Reality is actually pretty great. Everybody is doing something that they love and still able to come back to do the MxPx shows."

Sure, there were things they wished they'd done differently. Better marketing, better business planning (not something a punk band thought they'd have to focus much on), better legal advice, and all that. The fact that the band's members weren't millionaires many times over was hardly a failure. Yes, that they were changing the band's strategy after twenty-two years was, in some ways, proof that there are no guarantees in life. But in another way it's proof that, if you work hard, you will always have at least *some* success.

MxPx was a band that got to do what they loved for more than

---

* Mike actually released our conversation on his podcast and radio show—because he's expertly continued to build a platform for himself. You can listen to it here: http://mikeherrerabestlife.tumblr.com/post/134548508245/136-ryan-holiday-ryanholiday.

two decades—and from the looks of it, they will continue to pursue that love. They made more money than most bands could realistically dream of. They've done more than any artist can rightfully aspire to. Mike Herrera explained their reality to me: "If I were to realize that door A, B, or C all lead to a lot of heartache and pain, but you know, A was what I really want, well, why not just choose A?" He quoted Tom Petty to me: "Hey, baby, there ain't no easy way out." When it comes to making your art—whether it's music or writing or building a great company—you either really want it or you don't. There is no easy way in, or out.

When Kevin Kelly put forth his idea about having one thousand true fans, he wasn't saying you'd live like a king. He wasn't saying you wouldn't have to work hard, or that the struggle would be over. He was saying that you'd be able to *make a living*. He predicted that technology had made it possible to work and survive as an artist. Nowhere did he say that it would be easy or that you'd be filthy rich.

We didn't get into the creative business because it was *easy*, and we didn't get into it because of the certainties. In fact, most of us love this work because of the uncertainties, because that keeps it interesting. There remain many better, easier, less anxiety-producing ways to make money in this world. We didn't get into this business for that. We got into it because we didn't have a choice. We do what we do because there is nothing more rewarding than the artistic and creative process—even if those rewards aren't always financial, even if they don't accrue as quickly as we might have originally hoped.

At Mike Herrera's invitation, I saw MxPx play in San Antonio—almost fifteen years to the day after the first time I'd seen them play, as a teenager in a small venue near my hometown in Northern California. It was an incredible experience to see someone play the same songs with the same energy to a crowd significantly more diverse than I ever remembered. The show also happens to be part of an unbroken string of sold-out concerts the band has had since it started touring again. They just celebrated a quarter century as a group.

Mike and I became friends over time, and one afternoon, walking down the street in Seattle, we stopped in a vintage guitar store where Mike had bought a guitar many years earlier. The owner of the store recognized him. It'd been at least a decade since they'd seen each other, and he asked how things were going with the band. They talked about the group's long career. The owner beamed, his store having played a small role in it. Then the owner's son came out and began to gush: "You're Mike Herrera! From MxPx! I have all your records!"

This was the reason the owner had been excited—he'd heard his son listening to the music of a musician who'd once been to his store and gotten to impress his son in the way that all fathers ache to do. Mike, out for an ordinary afternoon walk, had bumped into the multigenerational impact of his work. He'd met a living, breathing embodiment of his perennial success. And I was lucky enough to be standing there and watching as these three people all experienced a tiny yet deeply personal moment that I can only imagine added meaning to the struggle that went into that success.

That's the truly fortunate part of being able to do creative work for a living. It's the best goddamn job in the world.

As for being lucky? The football coach Bill Walsh once explained the coaching strategy behind his Super Bowl–winning San Francisco 49ers as not being rooted in a relentless, aggressive pursuit of victory, but as something a little more counterintuitive— something that embraces the role of chance. After designing the right standards and assembling the right members for the team,

Walsh explained that his goal was to "establish a near-permanent 'base camp' near the summit, consistently close to the top, within striking distance." The actual probability of winning in a given year depended on a lot of external factors—injuries, schedule, drive, weather—just as it does for any mountain climber, for any author, for any filmmaker or entrepreneur or creative. We do know with certainty, however, that without the right preparation, there is zero chance of successfully making a run to the summit.

Walsh made three such summits in eight years with the 49ers. Was it preparation? Was it brilliance? Was it luck? It was all of these things assembled together.

It's that assemblage that we've attempted to formulize in this book.

In the first half, we focused on the standards for our products and projects. Making sure that we made something that put us within striking distance of the top—something close to the best in class for our field. We checked and rechecked and prepared ourselves.

The second half was about actually attempting that trip to the summit. It was about making our best effort on the ascent, knowing that there are no guarantees. Knowing that we'll need the right weather conditions and timely breaks to make it. How long it takes, how far we might get remains to be seen. But we're going to try—because that's who we are. This is what we do.

As for the uncertainty—that can't bother us. Because, as Arthur Miller wrote in *Death of a Salesman*, successfully fulfilling our creative need is "greater than hunger or sex or thirst, a need to leave a thumbprint somewhere on the world. A need for immortality, and by admitting it, the knowing that one has carefully inscribed one's name on a cake of ice on a hot July day."

Whether our imprint on the world lasts ten years as Cyril Connolly hoped for himself, or ten minutes or ten centuries, we cannot say. But we have to try to leave our mark nonetheless, and try not only once, but again and again.

When I asked Craig Newmark what it felt like to know that he had created something used by millions of people, something that's still going strong after twenty years, his answer was the perfect note to end this book on:

"It feels nice for a moment, then surreal, then back to work."

AFTERWORD

✸✸✸

C hatting with Judd Apatow about the trajectory of creative work after its release, Steve Martin once explained that there were three levels of "good" when it came to a movie: "One is when it comes out. Is it a hit? Then after five years. Where is it? Is it gone? Then again after ten [to] fifteen years if it's still around. Are people still watching it? Does it have an afterlife?"

As a book about how to make things that last, I hope my words will help other people create work that reaches each of Martin's three levels. Whether my words will last themselves, it's too early and presumptuous to even speculate. To paraphrase the Van Halen lyric, only time will tell whether this book, or any of the ideas we've talked about within it, stand the test of time.

If it doesn't, I hope to learn and improve accordingly. I won't have given up on the book by then; I can promise you that— certainly not after lecturing you on the importance of settling in for the long haul. Whatever the verdict, I know that the marks I've aimed for are worthwhile. I'm confident that the strategies in this book chart the best pathway to perennial success—even though, as with so many things in life, I can offer no guarantees. Regardless, I take great comfort and pride in the knowledge that you are now fully prepared to make and market a classic.

I look forward to checking back in with all of you in five, ten, and fifteen years. And hopefully many more decades after that.

A GIFT FOR YOU

❦

First off, thank you for taking the time to read and finish this book. As I discussed in the marketing section, deciding to read one book over another is a costly decision. Thank you for choosing this one. As an expression of my gratitude—and to follow my own advice in Part IV about building on our connection—I want to offer you something in return:

For a set of detailed case studies on books that I've worked on (which have sold millions of copies worldwide) plus additional, extended interviews with many of the brilliant experts quoted in this book, just send me an email at *hello@perennialseller.com.* You can also go to *perennialseller.com/gift.*

I hope we can continue this conversation about how to make work that lasts—and I hope to hear of any and all success you've had creating your own.

ACKNOWLEDGMENTS
AND SOURCES

I don't love the idea that we thank and acknowledge the friends and family who helped with a book but merely *list* our sources. For this book, I wanted to take the time to individually acknowledge and credit my sources, instead of listing them in some boring bibliography because they helped make this book a reality. Before I get to that, I'd also like to thank my partners at Brass Check, as well as our clients, especially Tim Ferriss, Robert Greene, and James Altucher, whose books and advice served as case studies. I want to thank my researcher, Hristo Vassilev, my editor, Niki Papadopoulos; thank you to Nils Parker and to my agent, Steve Hanselman. Thank you Portfolio for giving me the space and opportunity to create my own perennial sellers. Thank you to my wife, Samantha, for dealing with the piles of books all over the house and for my tendency to get lost inside them. I've been able to thank my pet goats in previous books, but now it's time to take it up a notch and thank my pet donkeys. Buddy and Sugar, I am watching you out the upstairs window as I write this. I'd thank my son, Clark, for his help, but to be perfectly honest he did not do anything to make this book possible.

Introduction

I owe a debt to Cyril Connolly, who served as the major breakthrough of this book and pivoted me away from a typical marketing book. The quotes about James Salter and Aleksandr Solzhenitsyn come from the back cover descriptions of their books. The quote about Bob Dylan comes from this CNN piece: cnn.com/2001/SHOWBIZ/Music/05/23 /dylan/. Here is a *Wall Street Journal* article on *The Shawshank Redemption*'s perennial success: wsj.com/articles/SB10001424052702 30453610457956002126555424o. Nils Parker found out about Cire Trudon and sent it my way. Nassim Taleb discusses the Lindy effect in his book *Antifragile*, and I also read the article "Lindy's Law" in *The New Republic* from June 1964. I'd known about Ted Turner's brilliant play with MGM but was reminded of it by a reader named Zach Grogan, who sent me a passage from *The Lion of Hollywood*. My editor sent me the news about catalog albums outselling new releases, which can be seen in this *Verge* article: theverge.com/2016/1/22/10816404/2015 -album-sales-trends-vinyl-catalog-streaming. The data on Tucker Max's book comes from Tucker, and I owe him a great deal for giving me my start—same too for Dov Charney.

Part I

Thanks to Derek Halpern and Pat Flynn, who helped kick off the Twitter discussion that opens this part. All quotes from Robert Greene come from an interview we did in 2015. Paul Graham's quote comes from this tweet: twitter.com/paulg/status/630132481732120576. The Sarah Silverman exchange is taken from her great appearance on Jerry Seinfeld's *Comedians in Cars Getting Coffee*. Casey Neistat's quote comes from his vlog (youtube.com/caseyneistatofficial) and then later a discussion we had. The line from Austin Kleon is from a tweet and newspaper blackout poem he did in 2015 (twitter.com/austinkleon /status/623940649025302528). You can watch Elon Musk discuss eating glass here: youtu.be/1NeqRhgtC10?t=42m51s and find Warren

Beatty's line about vomiting in this *New York Times* profile (nytimes .com/2016/10/30/movies/warren-beatty-rules-dont-apply.html). The Drake lyrics come from his song "Tuscan Leather" (and I owe thanks to his manager, Tony Hernandez, for the support). You can find more about Alexander Hamilton's writing style on page 250 of Ron Chernow's biography. The Stefan Zweig quote is in *The World of Yesterday*. The quote from Peter Thiel comes from his book *Zero to One*. The wonderful history of *Star Wars* is detailed in Cass Sunstein's book *The World According to Star Wars*, and the quotes from Rick Rubin come from his episode on the Tim Ferriss podcast (though we also had lunch in 2015—thank you, Neil Strauss—and discussed the same ideas). I've eaten at Clifton's Cafeteria many times and must thank them for the food. Joey Roth's design philosophy can be found in his 2009 interview with Boing Boing: boingboing.net/2009/10/19/joey -roth-on-design.html. The quote on *On the Road* comes from this article on NPR: npr.org/templates/story/story.php?storyId=11709924. One of the creativity studies referenced comes from 538.com, and thank you to Scott Barry Kaufman for agreeing to be interviewed. John Boyd's drawdown period can be found in Robert Coram's biography of the great man. Here's the piece where I found out about Frank Lucas's process: nymag.com/nymag/features/3649/#print. *Den of Geek* has a great piece on the early beginnings of Pixar movies here: denofgeek.com/movies/pixar/36648/the-early-versions-of-pixar -film-stories. Brian Koppelman has told his *Rounders* story many times, but one version can be found on his episode of the Tim Ferriss podcast. I owe my wife for buying *Worms Eat My Garbage*, and the Robert Evans quote comes from his autobiography. Paul Graham's essay is here: paulgraham.com/startupmistakes.html. Stephen King's quote about the ideal reader is from his book *On Writing*. Kurt Vonnegut's quote comes from his eight tips on how to write a great story, narrated here: youtube.com/watch?v=nmVcIhnvSx8. You can find the John Steinbeck quote here: theparisreview.org/interviews/4156 /john-steinbeck-the-art-of-fiction-no-45-continued-john-steinbeck.

Craig Newmark's quote comes from our e-mail interview done in 2015. Jon Favreau's quotes come from his interview with Marc Maron on the WTF podcast, and Albert Brooks's quote is taken from his interview with Judd Apatow for *Sick in the Head: Conversations About Life and Comedy*. Chigozie Obioma's piece can be read here: themillions.com/2015/06/the-audacity-of-prose.html. The numbers on Slayer's sales come from the book *Slayer's Reign in Blood*. Elizabeth Wurtzel's quote is from her short book *Creatocracy: How the Constitution Invented Hollywood*. Stephen King's "darlings" line is from *On Writing*. Robert McKee was nice enough to answer a few questions via email from me in 2015. I cannot recommend Pressfield's *The War of Art* highly enough.

Part II

The scene from John Fante's *Ask the Dust* is beautiful, and it remains one of my favorite works of fiction ever (thank you to Neil for turning me on to him). The biographical details about John Fante come from the biography *Full of Life* and basically everything about him ever written—my appetite for him is insatiable. Stats on YouTube are here: tubefilter.com/2015/07/26/youtube-400-hours-content-every-minute/ and stats on books published are here (bowker.com/news/2014/Tradi tional-Print-Book-Production-Dipped-Slightly-in-2013.html). I recommend this Jonathan Mahler article on Harper Lee's editor: nytimes .com/2015/07/13/books/the-invisible-hand-behind-harper-lees-to -kill-a-mockingbird.html; and this *Rolling Stone* piece about the creation of Adele's *25*: rollingstone.com/music/news/adele-inside-her -private-life-and-triumphant-return-20151103. I discovered Neil Gaiman's writing rules from this post by Maria Popova: brainpickings .org/2012/09/28/neil-gaiman-8-rules-of-writing/. Y Combinator's FAQ can be read here: ycombinator.com/faq/. James Altucher wrote a case study about writing, *Choose Yourself*, which you can read here: jamesaltucher.com/2013/07/how-to-self-publish-bestseller/. Max Martin's car test is detailed in *The Song Machine* by John Seabrook, and the Rolling Stones story is told in Rich Cohen's biography of the band, *The Sun & the Moon & the Rolling Stones.* (James Hetfield discussed his version of the test on the Joe Rogan podcast in 2016.) I've written more about Amazon's internal process in *Growth Hacker Marketing.* Brian Koppelman and Seth Godin discussed genre on Koppelman's podcast in 2016. Favreau is quoted again from the WTF podcast. The Justin's Peanut Butter quote came from a talk by Justin Gold at the Two12 conference in Boulder, Colorado, in 2016. Bret Taylor tells the story of Google Maps here: firstround.com/review /take-on-your-competition-with-these-lessons-from-google-maps/. Steve Jobs's six-figure logo story is in the Walter Isaacson bio, and Marissa Mayer's design testing is here: nytimes.com/2009/03/01 /business/01marissa.html. The fascinating story of Salinger's pulp cover is listed here: newyorker.com/magazine/2015/01/05/pulps-big -moment. You can read about the rebranding of *Edge of Tomorrow* here: variety.com/2014/film/news/tom-cruise-edge-of-tomorrow-gets -repositioned-as-live-die-repeat-on-home-video-1201283383/. Letters of Note has the Weinstein letter here: lettersofnote.com/2010/01 /youre-boring.html. The Seneca essay referenced is *On Tranquility.* The story of Snapper turning down Walmart is here: fastcompany .com/54763/man-who-said-no-wal-mart (though sadly they later reversed course). The Bruce Springsteen story comes from his book *Songs,* and Chuck Klosterman's quote is from his book *But What If We're Wrong?* Nabokov's quote is from *Vladimir Nabokov: Selected Letters 1940–1977* (in both cases I owe Austin Kleon for the heads-up). Jeff Goins's quote is from his forthcoming book, which I was lucky enough to work on. Kanye West's lyric is from the song "Run This Town." Churchill's struggle with writing and releasing is detailed in the first volume of *The Last Lion,* an epic masterpiece.

Part III

The Peter Thiel quote is from *Zero to One*. The Honoré de Balzac quote is from *Lost Illusions*. Herb Cohen is quoted by his son, Rich Cohen, in *The Sun & the Moon & the Rolling Stones*. "Marketing is anything that gets and keeps customers" appears in my book *Growth Hacker Marketing*. The Ian McEwan quote appears here: post-ga zette.com/ae/books/2013/03/24/A-conversation-with-Ian-Mc Ewan-on-the-hows-and-whys-of-fiction/stories/201303240168. Jason Fried was nice enough to be interviewed via phone in 2015. Byrd Leavell, who has represented a few projects I have ghostwritten or marketed, answered some of my questions via email in 2015. The Ries and Trout quote appears in *The 22 Immutable Laws of Marketing*. Ben Horowitz's line is from his book *The Hard Thing About Hard Things*. The Facebook statistic is from here: facebook.com/business/ news/Organic-Reach-on-Facebook. Shawn Coyne told me the story of their launch of *The Warrior Ethos* and provided the numbers. You can read about Bonobos's early days here: medium.com/@dunn/get -one-thing-right-89390244c553. The McKinsey study mentioned is here: mckinsey.com/insights/marketing_sales/a_new_way_to_measure _word-of-mouth_marketing. Jonah Berger's data is here: jonahberger .com/the-secret-science-behind-big-data-and-word-of-mouth/. I must thank Milt Deherrera for telling me about the Centralia coal-mine fire. Seth Godin's "sell one" comes from *Tribes*, changethis.com /manifesto/show/50.01.Tribes. I owe Austin Kleon again for the Padget Powell quote, and you can read the interview here: believermag.com /issues/200609/?read=interview_powell. The Truman Capote quotes are from *Capote: A Biography* and *Life* magazine's February 18, 1966, edition. I was made aware of the W. Somerset Maugham quote about posterity in Chuck Klosterman's *But What If We're Wrong?*, and I found a slightly different version. The story of 50 Cent is in *The 50th Law*, and I heard it directly from Robert Greene's interviews when I was a researcher. The "addicts" line is from a conversation I had with Shawn Coyne. Brady Dale, a writer I edit at the *Observer*, got those gems from Hugh Howey—the full interview is here: observer .com/2016/03/hugh-howey-wool-amazonkindle/. Tim Ferriss's quotes come from here: tim.blog/2013/05/02/a-few-thoughts-on-content-crea tion-monetization-and-strategy/. You can read the "Pretty Lights" story on *Hypebot*: hypebot.com/hypebot/2013/12/pretty-lights-gave -his-music-away-now-has-a-grammy-nomination-should-you-do -the-same.html. Paulo Coelho's thoughts on piracy are here: nytimes .com/2011/09/27/books/paulo-coelho-discusses-aleph-his-new -novel.html, and his Facebook post is here: facebook.com/paulo coelho/photos/a.241365541210.177295.11777366210/10153 068240216211/. The restaurant with the stolen pen is Texas Grill in Bastrop, Texas. Cory Doctorow discusses piracy here: publisher sweekly.com/pw/by-topic/columns-and-blogs/cory-doctorow/arti cle/55513-cory-doctorow-how-writers-lose-when-piracy-gets-harder .html. George Ouzounian (aka Maddox) was nice enough to do an email interview in 2016—my high school self never would have thought that would be possible. Andrew Meieran of Clifton's also did an email interview with me. My publisher argued with me quite a bit about Amazon's claim regarding ebook pricing, but I think the data is quite clear (price elasticity is also a fundamental law of economics). For more data, this *Observer* story is good: http://observer.com/2015 /09/do-e-books-earn-more-money-at-lower-prices. The *LA Times* has argued against it (http://www.latimes.com/books/jacketcopy /la-et-jc-amazon-e-book-numbers-20140731-story.html), but I think they come up short. Wrigley's price increase is here: articles.orlan dosentinel.com/1986-03-12/business/0200420078_1_chewing-gum -chewing-gum-wrigley. *The New Yorker* has a fascinating story on pulp fiction: newyorker.com/magazine/2015/01/05/pulps-big-moment. Raymond Chandler's quote about the overestimation of the impor- tance of literature to people is in *The Raymond Chandler Papers: Selected Letters and Nonfiction, 1909–1959*, and the numbers on his books sold are from *The Cambridge Companion to American Nov-*

elists. Thank you to BookBub.com for the discounted promotion and Tim Grahl for putting me onto it. *Thank you* to Neil Strauss for *Ask the Dust.* Drew Carey's story of his Carson nod is here: splitsider .com/2012/05/drew-carey-on-johnny-carsons-impact-on-stand-up -comedy/. My editor put me on to Kathy Sierra's concept of the "audience's audience," and it's told well in Sierra's talk "Creating Passionate Users," which you can watch here: youtu.be/eSlRd6MnDv8. Marc Ecko's swag bombs are discussed at length in his book *Unlabel.* (I was also lucky enough to work on that.) I must credit Samantha Weinman, Milt Deherrera, Nichole Williams, and Michelle Lemay for their work on fashion bloggers at American Apparel. George Raveling and Shaka Smart both told me the story about Calipari. Stories of paid excerpts are from *Robert Louis Stevenson: The Critical Heritage, F. Scott Fitzgerald on Authorship, The American Village in a Global Setting, Tom Wolfe: A Critical Companion,* and *Ray Bradbury: Uncensored!: The Unauthorized Biography.* You can read the *New York Times* profile of me here: nytimes.com/2016/12/06/fashion/ryan-holiday-sto icism-american-apparel.html, and the wedding announcement: ny times.com/2015/03/01/fashion/weddings/reclaiming-their-moment. html. The *20/20* story was titled "Faking It," and can be seen here: youtube.com/watch?v=p-7y1DohK5M. The *Sports Illustrated* piece is here: si.com/nfl/2015/12/08/ryan-holiday-nfl-stoicism-book-pete-carroll -bill-belichick, the podcast here: tombarnardpodcast.com/ryan-holi day-777-1/, and the blog post here: patriotsgab.com/2015/10/23/the-pa triots-2014-secret-weapon-may-have-been-a-book/. You can read about "trading up the chain" in this excerpt from *Trust Me, I'm Lying*: slide share.net/ryanholiday/tmil-slideshare-v19. Here's the *Times* piece on DeWitt service: nytimes.com/2013/06/24/us/in-the-bible-belt-offering -atheists-a-spiritual-home.html, and the Boing Boing piece by Zeds Dead: boingboing.net/2015/12/04/dj-duo-zeds-dead-stuck-heart-r.html. My Trump article is here: ryanholiday.net/dear-dad-dont-vote-don ald-trump/. Please read David Meerman Scott's book *Newsjacking.* Here is more about Amazon's drone stunt: cnbc.com/2013/12/02/did

-amazon-just-pull-off-the-best-pr-stunt-ever.html. *Adweek*'s piece is here: adweek.com/galleycat/author-experiments-with-genius-com -excerpt/106207. Jane Friedman's insight comes from an interview we did over the phone in 2015. Here is the history of the Koss Billboard: onmilwaukee.com/market/articles/kossbillboard.html. The Maxwell Perkins story is in A. Scott Berg's biography *Max Perkins: Editor of Genius*. H. L. Mencken's quote is from *Mencken: The American Iconoclast*. The 1985 *New York Times* piece on publishing is here: nytimes.com/1985/06/09/books/why-best-sellers-sell-best-and-other -publishing-secrets.html. Ian Fleming's advertising insights are in his wonderful book of letters, *The Man with the Golden Typewriter*. *The New Yorker* has the story of Patagonia's unusual ads: new yorker.com/business/currency/patagonias-anti-growth-strategy/. You can see my Times Square billboard here: instagram.com/p /BHAuZmEledp/. To be fair to the teachers at my high school—most were great. Here is Paulo Coelho's ad, which I love but am pissed he beat me to the punch: adweek.com/adfreak/paulo-coelho-just-pub lished-entire-text-his-novel-alchemist-single-ad-167068.

Part IV

Stefan Zweig's quote is from *The World of Yesterday*, and so is the sad story about his flight from Europe after the rise of Hitler. Iron Maiden's stats and stories come from countless sources (as you can tell I am infatuated with this band). There is currently no great biography of them, but there should be. Management turned down my requests for interviews. Please read Kevin Kelly's essay here: kk.org /thetechnium/1000-true-fans/. Michael Hyatt discusses platform in his book *Platform*. Winston Churchill's story is told in the second and third volumes of *The Last Lion*. I highly recommend Jackie Huba's book *Monster Loyalty*, on Lady Gaga. Marcus Aurelius's quote comes from *Meditations*. Casey Neistat and I discussed platform many times on runs up the West Side of Manhattan, and he has also mentioned it many times on his vlog. Kevin Hart tells the story of building his email list and social media on Marc Maron's WTF podcast, and the leaked Sony emails reveal more. Craig Newmark's quotes come from our interview. I also recommend Seth Godin's *Permission Marketing*. Chris Lavergne's quotes come from an email interview in 2015—thanks for all the support, my friend! I credit Ian Claudius for discouraging me from starting an email list—it's what made me do it. Thank you to Noah Kagan for his thoughts on building a list. Porter Gale wrote *Your Network Is Your Net Worth*. I'm so lucky to have met Tim Ferriss at SXSW, and thank you to Tucker Max for bringing me along as his assistant in 2007. Here are some of Tim's networking strategies: tim.blog/2015/08/26/how-to-build-a -world-class-network-in-record-time/. Jay Jay French's quote is from this article: inc.com/jay-jay-french/how-the-twisted-sister-brand-sur vive-for-five-decades.html. Thanks to Barbara Hendricks for doing an interview. Thanks to Robert Greene for suggesting I give *Structure of Scientific Revolutions* another chance many years ago. Here's a history of the book: theguardian.com/science/2012/aug/19/thom as-kuhn-structure-scientific-revolutions. The quote from Kafka's publisher is from this piece in *The New Yorker*: newyorker.com /books/page-turner/posthumous. Thanks to Steve Hanselman and Ralphie May for answering some questions. Thanks to Nassim Taleb for answering some questions on *Incerto* via email. The music study mentioned is here: chicagobooth.edu/research/workshops/Applied Econ/docs/Sorensen-Music.pdf. This piece on Woody Allen and the "writing life" is amazing: theimaginationgame.com/2012/12/18/writ ing-is-the-great-life-woody-allen/, as is this profile of Seinfeld: ny times.com/video/magazine/100000001965963/jerry-seinfeld-how-to -write-a-joke-.html. John McPhee's quotes are from here: chron.com /life/article/John-McPhee-isn-t-slowing-in-72nd-year-2123857.php. Goethe's line is from *Maxims and Reflections*. The hip-hop book I alluded to was with Birdman and Slim Williams, founders of Cash Money Records. The project is currently stalled, but I hope it picks up again. In regards to Michael Jackson's empire, read *Michael Jackson*

Inc. by Zack O'Malley Greenburg. Steven Johnson's piece on creativity in the *New York Times* is here: nytimes.com/2015/08/23/magazine /the-creative-apocalypse-that-wasnt.html. Jay Z's lyric is from his song "No Hook."

Conclusion and Afterword

The *Born to Run* story is from this interview with Bruce in *Rolling Stone*: http://www.rollingstone.com/music/news/bruce-springsteen-on-making-born-to-run-we-went-to-extremes-20150825. The MxPx documentary that precipitated my artistic crisis was *Both Ends Burning*. Thank you to Mike for the interview and for staying in touch—it's an unbelievable honor. The first time I saw MxPx play was a month after September 11th in Modesto, California. The Bill Walsh line is from *The Score Takes Care of Itself*. Nassim Taleb's quote is from this Boing Boing post: boingboing.net/2009/01/29/black-swan -authors-r.html. And thanks to Craig Newmark for the perfect end to the conclusion. And thank you to Judd Apatow because his interview with Steve Martin in *Sick in the Head* gave me the perfect way to end the book.

INDEX

❧

AC/DC, 212
Adele, 71, 72–73
advertising, 162–69
  best uses of, 167–69
  billboards, 165–66, 167–68
  product launch and, 125, 162
  T-shirts as free, 212
  using data for, 164
  word of mouth vs., 119
A Farewell to Arms (Hemingway), 38, 202
Agamemnon (Seneca), 100
Alchemist, The (Coelho), 169
Allen, Woody, 206–7, 214
Altucher, James, 75, 123–24, 160, 184, 189
Amazon
  paying employees to quit, 29
  potential audience on, 137–38
  sales rank, 117, 139–40, 149
  timelessness and, 31
Amazon Prime, 134
American Apparel, 9, 144, 145, 168
"amnesia marketing," 190
Apatow, Judd, 229
Appelhof, Mary, 44–45
Apple, 121, 128, 206

App Store, 154
AppSumo, 190
Ask the Dust (Fante), 63–65, 140–41, 219
audience
  defining intended, 44–47, 82–89
  "for what?" question, 47–51
  "audience's audience," 143
  availability bias, 33–34, 91
Avatar (movie), 28–29, 31n

"backtracking," 40
Basecamp, 112, 134, 204
Beatty, Warren, 25
Berger, Jonah, 119
Bezos, Jeff, 31
Bic pen, 137
Bitcoin, 160
BitTorrent, 132, 191
Blue Ocean Strategy, 52, 53
Bonfire of the Vanities, The (Wolfe), 150
book covers, 91–92, 94–95
Born to Run (album), 54, 103, 220–21
Bowie, David, 7
Boyd, John, 40
Bradbury, Ray, 135–36, 150
Brooks, Albert, 49

build a list, 184–92
Bukowski, Charles, 135–36, 141
BuzzFeed, 84

Cadaver Connection, 40
Cain, Susan, 84
Calipari, John, 147–48
"Call to Arms," 126
Cameron, James, 28–29
Campbell, Joseph, 34–35
Capote, Truman, 55, 56, 122, 122n
Carey, Drew, 141–42
Carroll, Pete, 53
Carson, Johnny, 141–42
car test, 76–77, 76n
Cash Money Records, 118
Catcher in the Rye, The (Salinger), 94–95
champions
    finding your, 140–43
    making the ask and utilizing, 143–48
    word of mouth and, 118–21
Chandler, Raymond, 138–39
Charity:water, 93–94
Choose Yourself (Altucher), 75, 123–24, 160, 184, 189
Churchill, Winston, 105, 180
Cire Trudon, 6
Clifton's Cafeteria (Los Angeles), 5, 35–36, 36, 135–36
Clinton, Hillary, 194–95, 195n
Coelho, Paulo, 131–32, 169
Cohen, Herb, 111
Cohen, Rich, 76–77
Connolly, Cyril, 1–2, 17, 38, 102, 118–19, 226–27
Contagious (Berger), 119n
contests, 191
core audience, 87, 152
Count of Monte Cristo, The (Dumas), 201
Coyne, Shawn, 88
Craigslist, 48, 157, 188, 203–4
creative process, 17–60
    bold, brash, and brave, 51–57
    building body of work, 204–9
    creativity, 37–39
    domain dominance, 44–47
    drawdown period, 40–41

"for what?" question, 47–51
    importance of the work, 19–21
    marathon vs. sprint, 27–29
    marketing vs. creating, 17–19
    role of ideas, 21–22
    role of purpose, 23–24
    short term vs. long term, 33–37
    testing ideas, 41–44
    timelessness, 29–32
    willingness to sacrifice, 24–27
Cruise, Tom, 37, 95
Curtis, Drew, 187

Daily Stoic, The (Holiday), 216
Darabont, Frank, 37
Death of a Salesman (Miller), 226
De Vany, Arthur, 205n
DeWitt, Jerry, 156
Dickinson, Bruce, 214
"Dip, the" (Godin), 28
discovery costs, 129
Doctorow, Cory, 132–33
domain dominance, 44–47
"Don't Buy This Jacket" ad, 167
drafts, 25, 70, 76–77
Drake, 29
drawdown period, 40–41
Drucker, Peter, 113
Dumas, Alexandre, 201, 209n
Dylan, Bob, 3

ebooks, 138, 139
Ecko, Marc, 103, 144
Ecko Unltd., 144
Edge of Tomorrow (movie), 95
editors, role of, 69–76, 82
elevator pitch, 97
email lists, 184–92
    how to build, 188–92, 196
    Kevin Hart's platform, 185–87
    use of email, 187–88
empire building, 211–16
endorsements (endorsers)
    finding, 140–43
    making the ask and utilizing, 143–48
    word of mouth and, 118–21
Enemies of Promise (Connolly), 1–2, 17, 102, 118–19
entrepreneurial mindset, 212–13

Epictetus, 170
Evans, Robert, 44
Evernote, 20

Fahrenheit 451 (Bradbury), 150
fans, 197–99
   reaching out to new, 209–11
Fante, John, 63–65, 140–41, 219
Favreau, Jon, 49–50, 80–81
feedback, 42, 69–76
Ferriss, Tim, 92, 129, 192–94
50 Cent, 127–28, 131, 134, 160, 209
Fitzgerald, F. Scott, 73, 149–50, 163
Fleming, Ian, 165, 202–3, 215
Fog of War, The (documentary), 96
4-Hour Workweek, The (Ferriss), 92
48 Laws of Power, The (Greene), 8–9
free marketing strategy, 127–35, 190
freemium, 134, 171
French, Jay Jay, 197
Fried, Jason, 112
Friedman, Jane, 161

Gaiman, Neil, 73
Game, The (Strauss), 202
genre, 79–81
Godin, Seth, 28, 68, 80, 120, 188, 200–201
Goethe, Johann Wolfgang von, 52–53, 210
Goins, Jeff, 104
Google, 32, 33, 92, 215
Google Alert, 148
Google Doodles, 160–61
GoreTex, 50
Graham, Paul, 20, 46
Grateful Dead, 53
Great Gatsby, The (Fitzgerald), 8, 73
Greene, Robert, 20, 88–89
   annotating excerpts, 160
   The Art of Seduction, 202
   body of work, 205, 209
   The 48 Laws of Power, 8–9
   Mastery, 89, 133n

Hamilton, Alexander, 30–31
Hanselman, Stephen, 202–3
"Happy Birthday" (song), 51
Hart, Kevin, 185–87

Hefner, Hugh, 150
Hemingway, Ernest, 37, 38, 70, 163, 202, 214
Hendricks, Barbara, 198, 200
Hendricks, Ken, 206
Henley, Don, 144
Herrera, Mike, 223–25
Hetfield, James, 76n
Hidden Fortress, The (movie), 34
History of the English-Speaking Peoples, A (Churchill), 105
Hitler, Adolf, 65
Hohoff, Tay, 70–72
Horowitz, Ben, 116
Howey, Hugh, 129
Huba, Jackie, 181n
humility, 41–42, 75, 114–16
Hyatt, Michael, 179, 180

ideas
   drawdown period, 40–41
   as a lightning strike, 38
   role of, 21–22, 52
   testing, 41–44
I Hope They Serve Beer in Hell (Max), 8–9, 131
In Cold Blood (Capote), 55, 56, 122n
influencers
   finding your, 140–43
   making the ask and utilizing, 143–48
   word of mouth and, 118–21
Instagram, 141
   "Stories" feature, 169–70
Iron Maiden, 5, 176–79, 184, 214
   fan base, 176–79, 197
   T-shirt sales, 212
Iron Man (movie), 49–50, 80–81

Jackson, Michael, 212
Jagger, Mick, 76–77
Jay Z, 118, 211, 213, 216
Jenkins, Jerry, 48
Jobs, Steve, 92, 102, 206
Johnson, Steven, 213
Justin's Peanut Butter, 87

Kafka, Franz, 202
Kagan, Noah, 190, 191
karmic debt, 196, 198–99

Katz's Deli, 50, 147
Kaufman, Scott Barry, 38–39
Keats, John, 39
Kelly, Kevin, 178, 224
Kerouac, Jack, 38, 38n, 135
Keynes, John Maynard, 121
Kim, W. Chan, 52
King, Stephen, 46–47, 58
Kleon, Austin, 22, 121n
Klosterman, Chuck, 103
Knight, Phil, 118
Kogi Korean BBQ, 43
Kool DJ Red Alert, 144
Koppelman, Brian, 42, 80
Koss Corporation, 165–66
Kuhn, Thomas, 199

Lady Gaga, 5n, 87, 181, 197, 209
Lamott, Anne, 43
Langer's Deli, 50
La Sagrada Família (Barcelona), 27
launch, the, 120–27, 202
   the "what," 125–27
Lavergne, Chris, 188
Leavell, Byrd, 112
Lee, Harper, 70–72, 208
Lee, Spike, 144
Levien, David, 42
Lewis, Sinclair, 150
Libin, Phil, 20
Life (magazine), 150
Lindy effect, 6, 117, 187, 198–99
Litt, Toby, 46
Louis C.K., 207, 210
Lucas, Frank, 40
Lucas, George, 8, 25, 34–35

McEwan, Ian, 111
McKee, Robert, 58–59
McPhee, John, 25n, 208
Mad Men (TV show), 27–28
Marcus Aurelius, 97, 184
marketing, 109–71, 203–4
   advertising, 162–69
   anything can be, 116–18
   building body of work, 204–9
   cheap strategy, 135–41
   creating vs., 17–19
   finding champions, 140–43

free strategy, 127–35
   as a job, 111–14
   the launch, 120–27
   making the ask, 143–48
   media coverage, 148–59
   newsjacking, 159–62
   reaching out to new fans, 209–11
   sense of entitlement, 114–16
   word of mouth, 118–21
Maron, Marc, 195
Martin, Max, 76, 76n, 77
Martin, Steve, 229
Mastery (Greene), 89, 133n
Mauborgne, Renée, 52
Maugham, W. Somerset, 122
Max, Tucker, 9, 131
May, Ralphie, 202
Mayer, Marissa, 92
media coverage, 148–59
   credibility and status, 150–51
   grabbing attention, 154–59
   newsjacking, 159–62
   paid (advertising), 162–69
   starting small, 152–54
Meieran, Andrew, 35, 135–36
Mein Kampf (Hitler), 65
Melville, Herman, 206
Mencken, H. L., 163n
Metallica, 76n, 132, 134, 212
Miller, Arthur, 226
Minimum Viable Product, 43
Miranda, Lin-Manuel, 45
Monster Loyalty (Huba), 181n
Monsters, Inc. (movie), 50
Morris, Errol, 96
Musk, Elon, 25, 99
MxPx, 221–25

Nabokov, Vladimir, 103
Nas, 146
Neistat, Casey, 21–22, 158, 182–83, 189
network, as net worth, 192–94
New England Patriots, 153
Newmark, Craig, 48, 188, 227
newsjacking, 159–62
   advertising and, 168
newsletters, 189, 192
NeXT, 92
Nike, 118, 128

Obioma, Chigozie, 54
Obstacle Is the Way, The (Holiday),
    139, 152–53, 166
Once a Runner (Parker), 118
"One for Them, One for Me" strategy,
    210
"One Sentence, One Paragraph, One
    Page" exercise, 78–82, 96–97
1,000 True Fans, 178, 224
On the Road (Kerouac), 38, 38n, 135
Orbison, Roy, 95
O'Reilly, Tim, 128
Original Pantry Cafe (Los Angeles), 5,
    204
Orwell, George, 24–25
Ouzounian, George, 134–35

packaging, 90–98
Page, Larry, 32
paid media, 162–69
paradigm shifts, 199
Parker, John, Jr., 118
Patagonia, 167
Patterson, James, 157
Peretti, Jonah, 84
Perkins, Maxwell, 163
"permission assets," 188
piracy, 128, 131–32, 134
pitch, the, 90–91, 95–98
platform, 175–217
    building a body of work, 204–9
    building an empire, 211–16
    building your list, 184–92
    defined, 179–82
    importance of, 182–84
    marketing, 203–4
    network, 192–94
    reaching out to new fans, 209–11
    relationships, 194–99
    settling in for long haul, 199–203
positioning, 63–106
    audience question, 82–89
    CEO of work, 67–69
    commercialism, 102–4
    halfway to halfway point, 66–67
    mission, 98–102
    "One Sentence, One Paragraph, One
        Page," 78–82
    packaging and the pitch, 90–98

role of editors, 69–76
    testing and retesting, 76–77
Powell, Padgett, 120–21
Presley, Elvis, 88, 211
Pressfield, Steven, 59, 116–17
pre-VIPs, 193–94
pricing
    cheap strategy, 135–41
    freemium, 134, 171
    free strategy, 127–35
Pullman, Bill, 6–7
pulp paperbacks, 138–39

Quiet (Cain), 84

Rao, Srinivas, 53
Rap Genius, 160
Ray-Ban Wayfarers, 144
Reign in Blood (album), 55
Ries, Al, 93, 113
Rocky (movie), 37, 38
Rolling Stones, 76–77
Roth, Joey, 36, 140
Rounders (movie), 42
Rubin, Rick, 35, 54–55, 72

Salinger, J. D., 94–95
Salter, James, 2–3
Sanders, Bernie, 194–95
Schwarzenegger, Arnold, 182
Scott, David Meerman, 159
Scribner's Magazine, 149
Seinfeld (TV show), 31, 91, 207
Seinfeld, Jerry, 207, 210
Seneca, 100
serialized novels, 149–50
Sex and the City (TV show), 87
Shakespeare, William, 8, 205
Shawshank Redemption, The (movie),
    4–5, 37
Siegler, M. G., 154
Sierra, Kathy, 143
Silverman, Sarah, 21
Sistine Chapel, 27
Slaughterhouse-Five (Vonnegut), 119n
Slayer, 54–55
Smith, Derek Vincent (aka Pretty
    Lights), 129–30
Snapchat, 170

Snapper Inc., 101
social media, 169–70, 187
    "Call to Arms," 126
social proof, 147–48
Solzhenitsyn, Aleksandr, 3
Sorapot, 36, 140
Soulja Boy, 131
South by Southwest (SXSW), 157, 193
spontaneous creation, myth of, 37–39,
    57–58
Sports Illustrated, 153, 166
Spotify, 5, 110, 134, 209
Springsteen, Bruce, 54, 103, 220–21
startups
    growth rate, 20
    market need, 48, 49n
    Minimum Viable Product, 43
    reason for failure, 48n
    short term vs. long term, 34
starving artists, 104
Star Wars (movies), 7–8, 25, 34–35, 122,
    182, 201n
Steinbeck, John, 47, 214
Stevenson, Robert Louis, 149
Strauss, Neil, 92, 141, 168n, 202
Structure of Scientific Revolutions, The
    (Kuhn), 199
Sunstein, Cass, 122
"swag bomb," 144

Taleb, Nassim, 6, 205, 220
Taylor, Bret, 91
TED Talks, 129, 130
Thiel, Peter, 33, 109, 112
Thin Blue Line, The (movie), 96
Thompson, Hunter S., 25
To Kill a Mockingbird (Lee), 70–72
Tonight Show, The (TV show), 141–42
Toyota Way, 30
Toy Story (movie), 50
"trading up the chain," 153
Trout, Jack, 93, 113
Trust Me, I'm Lying (Holiday), 85–86,
    99

Truth, The (Strauss), 92
Turner, Ted, 7
22 Immutable Laws of Marketing, The
    (Ries and Trout), 93
Twisted Sister, 197
Twitter, 18, 186, 204

Uber, 55, 209

Van Halen, 229
Van Hofwegen, Nick, 214–15
Vonnegut, Kurt, 47, 119n

Walmart, 101, 163
Walsh, Bill, 225–26
War of Art, The (Pressfield), 59
War of the Worlds, The (radio
    broadcast), 55, 56
Warrior Ethos, The (Pressfield), 116–17
WD-40, 50, 73
Wealthfront, 95
Weiner, Matthew, 27–28
Weinstein, Harvey, 95–96
Weintraub, Jerry, 88
Welch, Jack, 198, 207
Welles, Orson, 55, 56, 57
West, Kanye, 104, 144, 209
Wolfe, Tom, 150
Wool (Howey), 129
word of mouth, 118–21, 170
Worms Eat My Garbage (Appelhof),
    44–45
Wrecker, The (Stevenson), 149
Wrigley's gum, 137
Wurtzel, Elizabeth, 56

Y Combinator, 20, 46, 68, 73–74
YouTube, 68, 183, 189

Zappos, 29
Zeds Dead, 156–57
Zero to One (Thiel), 112
Zildjian cymbals, 5–6
Zweig, Stefan, 32, 175, 180–81